Versailles: The View from Sweden

Versailles: The View from Sweden

Elaine Evans Dee and Guy Walton

Cooper-Hewitt Museum

The Smithsonian Institution's National Museum of Design

Cooper-Hewitt Museum
2 East 91st Street
New York, New York 10128

LC 87-073539
ISBN 0-910503-56-7

Edited by Nancy Aakre with Joanna Ekman
Designed by H +
Typeset by Trufont Typographers, Inc.
Printed in the United States by Rembrandt Press, Inc.

Library of Congress Cataloging-in-Publication Data

Dee, Elaine Evans.
  Versailles : the view from Sweden.

  Exhibition catalog.
  Bibliography: p.
  1. Tessin, Nicodemus, 1659–1728—Exhibitions.
2. Architectural drawing—17th century—Sweden—Exhibitions.
3. Architectural drawing—18th century—Sweden—Exhibitions.
4. Architectural drawing—17th century—France—Exhibitions.
5. Château de Versailles (Versailles, France)—Designs and plans—
Exhibitions.   6. Interior architecture—France—Versailles—
Exhibitions.   7. France—Social life and customs—17th–18th
centuries—Exhibitions.   8. Versailles (France)—Description—
Views—Exhibitions.   I. Walton, Guy.   II. Cooper-Hewitt
Museum.   III. Title.
NA2707.T47A4   1988   720′.22′2   87-73539
ISBN 0-910503-56-7

Contents

Foreword Harold F. Pfister   6

Versailles: The View from Sweden Elaine Evans Dee   9

The Versailles Drawings in Stockholm Guy Walton   14

Catalogue   17

Foreword

Versailles was, and remains, more than a mere palace. Named for the village where the hunting lodge at its core was first constructed, this sprawling complex of buildings and gardens became Europe's synonym for the unprecedented cultural might of the French monarchy. Nowhere else had a single monarch so centralized and personalized the government of the modern nation-state, and nowhere else had the philosophy of absolutism received such pervasive and breathtaking visualization. If architecture is about power—and it is—the architectural triumph of Versailles also surely drew much of its total impact from the contributions of the many related arts that covered its surfaces, arranged and adorned its grounds, produced its furnishings, ornaments, fittings, conveyances and personal objects of daily use, costumed its court and choreographed its intricate rituals of social intercourse. The unity of the arts at Versailles, with architecture foremost, stood as a tangible metaphor for the well-ordered unity of the kingdom itself, with Louis XIV at its head.

Modern readers may wonder at the king's personal interest in the geography of bedchambers designed for members of his family or in the symbolism of the chapel in which their prayers were to be collectively offered. But details of such plans reflect the vital significance of the entire complex for the monarch's ambitions and methods of governance, and precisely such details animate the majority of sheets selected for *Versailles: The View from Sweden*.

Particularly during the adventurous reign of Charles XII, a militant personality bold enough to lead his formidable troops into a doomed conflict with the Russia of Peter the Great, Sweden seems to have been an especially responsive and admiring observer of Louis XIV's performance as monarch and patron. As the exhibition clearly demonstrates, the northern kingdom's leading talents learned what they could from the established architectural traditions of their southern neighbors, Italy in particular. Perhaps inevitably, however, they and their royal patrons could scarcely imagine a more impressive, all-encompassing deployment of their energies and abilities than in well-studied emulations of Louis's contemporary accomplishments at Versailles.

Image making among national leaders is hardly the invention of electronic journalism. The documents in this exhibition, apart from their inherent beauty, are eloquent reminders of how power has sought to proclaim itself; how cultures have observed and interacted with each other; how propaganda has entered the lives of nations, shaped the experiences of individuals, and ultimately become part of a shared and affecting heritage that long survives its progenitors. The drawings thus invite, and amply repay, the closest and most thoughtful scrutiny we can give them.

The Cooper-Hewitt Museum acknowledges with profound gratitude the many professional courtesies extended to us by Per Bjurström, Director of the Nationalmuseum in Stockholm, and Börje Magnusson, Curator of Drawings and Prints at that museum, which has lent the majority of the drawings on view. Additional loans were made available most graciously from the Royal Palace and from the Wasasamlingen in Stockholm; for their assistance, we thank Ragnar Jonsson and Axel Norberg, respectively. Beate Sydhoff, cultural counselor of the Swedish embassy in Washington, D.C., has facilitated our communications with colleagues and sponsors in Sweden, and we are in her debt for her kindness and efficiency in that role.

This publication would not have been possible without the handsome support of The Port Royal Foundation, Inc. Research for the exhibition was assisted, in part, by a grant from the Svenska Institutet in Stockholm, and international air transport was generously provided by Scandinavian Airlines, through the auspices of New Sweden '88. All of these sponsors, as well as the friends of the Cooper-Hewitt, whose support has defrayed additional related expenses, have our sincere thanks.

Elaine Evans Dee, Curator of Drawings and Prints at the Cooper-Hewitt, selected the drawings for the exhibition and worked hard and long to assure this publication's appearance. Guy Walton, Professor of Fine Arts at New York University, to whom we turned for much of the catalogue material, was the scholar who convinced us that the entire project was possible. We hope he is as pleased as we are with the results of his interest and efforts.

Harold Francis Pfister
Acting Director

Versailles: Cour de Marbre and Château; etching and engraving; Israël Silvestre (1621–1691)

Versailles: Château from the Gardens; etching and engraving; Israël Silvestre (1621–1691)

Versailles: The View from Sweden

Louis XIV's Versailles was a fusion of the arts, of political and social events, and of the will of the monarch. It was the showpiece of Europe, and Sweden was its most appreciative and enthusiastic audience. The Swedish monarchs sent emissaries, most notably their extraordinary architect Nicodemus Tessin the Younger, to observe in detail the buildings, the gardens, the furnishings, and the activities at Versailles in order to keep them informed of the latest styles at the French court. Like every other monarch in Europe, the Swedish crown wished to emulate at home the grandeur that Versailles exemplified.

The transformation of Versailles from a red brick and white stone hunting lodge to an imposing royal residence and seat of government, from a rural retreat to a center for music, theater, architecture, gardens, paintings, sculpture, and the decorative arts was the greatest achievement of Louis XIV's long reign (1661–1715). That the building of the château of Versailles, its decoration, and its furnishing were even possible was a triumph of French genius, as these undertakings coincided with the king's career of conquest. Louis's ambition to make France the most powerful country in Europe embroiled his kingdom in four major military campaigns between 1667 and 1714, with the result that the royal building budget constantly competed with the nation's military expenditure. Nor was Versailles Louis's only architectural endeavor: many other constructions were considered or accomplished. The extension of the Louvre Palace was an immense, ongoing project involving numerous architects. The Tuileries Palace, the châteaus of Saint Germain-en-Laye, Chambord, and Fontainebleau were reconstructed or redecorated, and Clagny was built. While the king was at work, other members of the royal family were actively constructing or refurbishing residences in the country and in Paris, as well.

An administrative apparatus and the systematic development of artistic talent were the foundations of Louis's achievement in the arts. To accomplish the construction of the château of Versailles with its gardens, pavilions, and service buildings during unsettled times required efficiency and planning, qualities that Louis demanded of his staff. The king made wise choices of intelligent and talented people for key posts. Jean-Baptiste Colbert (1619–1683), while performing his duties as the minister of finance, was at the same time capable of assuming the office of superintendent of the king's building works, and in this capacity supervised the royal architect Jules Hardouin-Mansart (1646–1708), who held this post from 1678 to 1699. The first architect in turn commanded a battery of architects, specialized designers, draftsmen, and engineers to complete the seemingly endless building projects. Charles Le Brun (1619–1690), the first painter to the king, was also enlisted as an administrator and designer in 1663, when he was appointed director of the Manufacture Royale des Meubles de la Couronne established at the Gobelins manufactory. He directed not only tapestry weavers, but painters, sculptors, silversmiths, and cabinetmakers. Foreign artisans were imported when necessary to teach skills undeveloped in France such as lace- and glassmaking. The office of the *menus plaisirs*, where the designing of the all-important festivities of the court took place, was greatly expanded. It was administered by the king's designer-draftsman, Jean I Berain (1640–1711). The king accepted only the best, and to meet this challenge, those he employed were stretched to produce their finest work. He was interested in every detail of the planning of the buildings, including their interior decoration, and of the gardens, and he personally accepted or rejected all designs.

Versailles was remarkable not only because Louis XIV and his staff were able to visualize and then build a huge château and vast garden, but also because the design and execution throughout was of the highest standard of craftsmanship. The Gobelins was established to maintain this high standard in the furnishings supplied to the royal houses. Although it was Colbert's intention to sell abroad the luxury goods produced here and elsewhere—linens, lace, silks, tapestry, carpets, glass, ceramics, metalwork, and furniture—it appears that the demands of the French royal family absorbed most of the production of their own manufactories.

The monarchs of Europe, impressed by such accomplishments in the arts, were no less fascinated by the conduct of the court at Versailles. The king's relationship to the members of his court became a model for others to follow. Louis XIV established a system of etiquette by means of which he emphasized his position as ruler and his control of the nobility, and at Versailles the regimen of daily life was minutely observed. The king was on public view nearly all of his waking hours, and Versailles was created with the idea of providing this very visible person with grandly ceremonial surroundings at all times. The arrangement of the rooms at Versailles, for instance, stressed the public rather than the private life of the king. The gardens, the setting for lavish spectacles with concerts, ballets, operas, theatrical performances, and fireworks to celebrate births and weddings or simply as week-long diversions from more serious occupations, were also conceived for propagandistic purposes. The king himself wrote a guide for touring the gardens, naming specific stopping points, particularly for viewing the splendid water displays. As members of the court or guests strolled along the miles of paths, the iconographic program of sculpture, fountains, and ironwork blatantly proclaimed or subtly implied the power of the Sun King by relating him to the mythological figure of Apollo, the sun god. Other monarchs, who could not fail to be impressed by the sumptuousness and elegance of Versailles, were aware also that it created an atmosphere that enhanced the prestige of the king. Each longed to build a similar architectural wonder for himself, and the Swedish king regarded Versailles with particular admiration.

Sweden was a leading Baltic power by the first quarter of the seventeenth century, and after the Thirty Years' War (1618–48) it was acknowledged to be a great military power in Europe. Under Charles XI (1655–1697), a strong autocratic monarchy emerged that was highly susceptible to the allure of the court of Louis XIV. Prosperous and secure, the Swedish monarchy embarked on numerous building projects. After 1660 these were under the able direction of the royal architect, Nicodemus Tessin the Elder (1625–1681), whose best-known work is the palace at Drottningholm. His son Nicodemus Tessin the Younger (1654–1728), after studying architecture with his father, made several lengthy visits to Europe (Italy and other countries, 1673–77; France, 1677–80 and again 1687–88). His travels are an indication of the need felt by the young architect and his royal patrons for firsthand knowledge of architecture and design outside Sweden. The younger Tessin's studies in Italy left him with a lifelong admiration for the architecture of antique Rome, the Renaissance, and the baroque; he was particularly impressed by Michelangelo and he revered Bernini, whom he met. In France, he was not content to view French art, but made a point of establishing personal relationships with French artists. He met engravers, several of whom he later employed to reproduce his own works. Most important for the future of Swedish architecture and design was his friendship with the designer Jean I Berain, the sculptor François Girardon (1628–1715), and the garden designer André Le

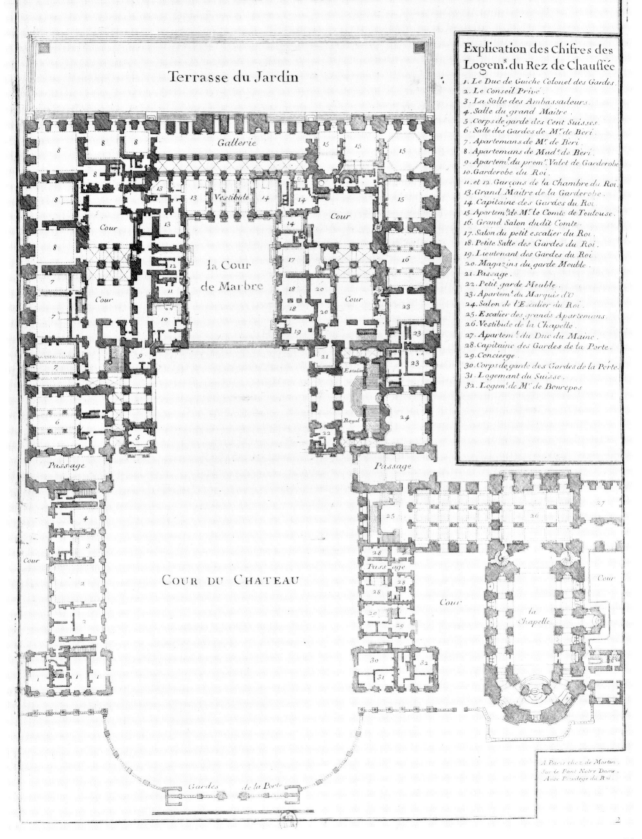

PLAN DU REZ DE CHAUSSÉE DU CHATEAU ROYAL DE VERSAILLES.

Stockholm, Royal Palace: View from the Northeast; engraving; Johan Eric Rehn (1717–1793) after Carl Palmcrantz (1694–1715)

Nôtre (1613–1700). He was able to study the drawings in the archives of the royal workshops and to observe the work of Charles Le Brun. It became Tessin's ambition to organize in Sweden an administration for art and architecture similar to the French system, with himself at the top. Eventually, Berain and Girardon were helpful in Tessin's search for good artists who were willing to spend time in Sweden carrying out the decorating of buildings there.

On Tessin's first visit to France, from 1677 to 1680, he felt that he profited most from studying the work of Le Nôtre for the Versailles gardens. At this time the gardens were at a more advanced stage than the château. (While Tessin could have seen portions of the lower floors, the upper apartments would not have been adequately finished.) Upon his father's death in 1681, Tessin became involved in completing the gardens at Drottningholm. Armed with copious notes and many drawings he had made of Le Nôtre's designs, the young architect prepared his plan for the gardens, recalling the lessons he had learned in France. Over thirty years later Tessin would remember the long allée at Versailles and the importance of the water pools and fountains when he submitted plans to Charles XII (ruled 1697–1718) for a country palace.

On Tessin's second visit, in 1687, he saw Versailles at the moment of maximum splendor. The brilliantly painted and stuccoed ceilings of the rooms, the walls covered in patterned red or green velvet embroidered with gold thread over which great paintings were hung, the floors paved with different colored marbles, and the furniture of gleaming silver or of inlaid woods and gilt bronze, all must have been impressive. Tessin's response to this French experience was unreserved enthusiasm for the brilliant and magnificent court of Louis XIV. The architect was much flattered by the French. Louis even honored Tessin by playing all the fountains at Versailles for him while the court was present—a compliment that was not taken lightly. Tessin's privileged position was based on the French perception that he might be able to influence the Swedish king to strengthen the political alliance with France.

In Nicodemus Tessin the Younger, the Swedish

royal family had found the ideal person to act as a bridge between Versailles and Stockholm. He was dedicated in his desire to serve his rulers and to make their surroundings and the structure of their lives as elegant as everything he had seen at Versailles. He was energetic, ambitious, intelligent, and highly organized, and his journals, letters, notes, and drawings reveal an acute observer. In his monumental vision for Sweden and for the capital city of Stockholm in particular, no project was too complex; he even submitted a plan to Charles XII for the complete rebuilding of the city in the area near the Royal Palace. The strength of his drive toward the perfection he saw as Versailles carried along not only the architects and draftsmen in his workshop, but all the French and Swedish artisans who were associated with his work.

In Tessin's own buildings, the lessons learned in Italy and France were important. He revered the power and unity, as he described it, of Italian architecture, and he admired the richness of Le Brun's interiors, the extraordinary patterns of Le Nôtre's gardens, and the monumentality of Girardon's sculpture. He strove to capture the same qualities in Swedish buildings.

At the grandiose Royal Palace in Stockholm, Tessin aimed to achieve the sumptuous, elegant, and stately atmosphere that prevailed at Versailles. The arrangement of rooms, particularly the ceremonial ones, was based on French practice. Tessin found it necessary to import French painters and sculptors to effect his designs for the ornamentation of rooms, but he very specifically stated that drawings would be provided to them. His decorative compositions combined arabesques, strapwork, vase shapes and sculptural, plastic figures in a way not seen in France, although the influence is clear.

This brilliant era for Sweden came to an end in 1721, when its armies were defeated and its treasuries depleted through the obsessive policy of aggression under Charles XII. Sweden withdrew from the center of the European political arena, and royal architectural projects were set aside for lack of funds. Work on the Royal Palace stopped completely. Only in 1728, the last year of his life, was Tessin given the satisfaction of seeing new funds appropriated to complete the palace on which he had labored with such loyalty.

Nicodemus Tessin the Younger was the conduit for bringing French ideas to Sweden, but he served a royal family whose aspirations to emulate the triumphant French court were comparable to his own. When this Swedish architect reached the stage in his career that he had sufficient confidence to send the king of France serious designs for projects so monumental as the expansion of the Louvre and so elaborate and personal as the Apollo Pavilion for Versailles, Swedish design had come of age.

Elaine Evans Dee
Cooper-Hewitt Museum

The Versailles Drawings in Stockholm

About two hundred sheets depicting the château, gardens, town, and interior decoration of Versailles can be identified in Stockholm's Nationalmuseum collection. The interest of these drawings lies in the fact that they were collected by the Swedish royal architects at precisely the time that many of the buildings, objects, and gardens shown were created. Furthermore, the Swedes were in a unique position to gain access to this material in the years between about 1680 and 1740. During this period Sweden was either an important political ally of France or the French were actively seeking a close connection with that kingdom. The arts professionals of the Swedish court were always welcome in France, and they regularly visited Paris and Versailles to keep abreast of innovations both in design and in the technology related to architecture, gardens, theater, and garden fêtes. The drawings acquired by the Swedish royal architects on their travels eventually came to the Nationalmuseum.

Queen Hedvig Eleonora (1635–1715), the builder of Drottningholm Palace and a patroness of the arts, arranged for a lengthy visit to France for the son of her principal architect, Nicodemus Tessin the Elder, during the young man's study years in the 1670s. It is possible that the Nationalmuseum collection of Versailles drawings began at that time, though it has proved impossible to identify with certainty any drawings acquired then. An important group was definitely assembled in 1687, during a second long visit to France by Tessin the Younger after he had succeeded his father as the Swedish royal architect. Tessin's well-known journal from this trip survives (reprinted in 1926 in *Revue de l'histoire de Versailles*, it is an interesting source of information on the arts in the France of this period), and a number of views and plans of places and objects drawn by Tessin to illustrate his notes can be identified (see Nos. 76 and 77). Two other types of drawings also seem to have been acquired. Some drawings from the workshops of the French king were probably received as gifts or were purchased. Other sheets would seem to date precisely to the time of the Tessin visit and may have been made by draftsmen other than those recognizable as employed by the French king (see No. 1). It seems that during his visit the architect commissioned a number of careful studies from French independent draftsmen to add to his files.

In Tessin's view it was necessary for the designer of a king whose country was a major European military power to work according to the best contemporary standards of both France and Italy. In order to supplement the information gathered on his travels, he attempted to acquire systematically illustrations of what was new and interesting abroad to take back to Stockholm. This pursuit amounted to the careful accumulation of what is a great collection of prints. Tens of thousands of these works, now divided between the Nationalmuseum and the Royal Library, survive. Many remain in the albums in which they were arranged by the architect himself to serve as a study resource; they were grouped according to subject matter, so that there are volumes of costumes, set designs, catafalques, and so on.

The drawings that Tessin collected were far less numerous and were specifically intended to fill gaps in the information provided by the prints, since not every important design was engraved and, furthermore, it was often years before sets of engravings were completed. Some kinds of objects, such as important table silver, were never engraved. The relationship of the prints to the drawings in Tessin's collection is clearly indicated in his *Catalogue des Livres, Estampes et Desseins du Cabinet des Beaux Arts et des Sciences Appartenant au Baron Tessin*, which he published in Stockholm during 1712.

The collecting achievement celebrated in Tessin's catalogue was substantially due to the architect's decision in 1693 to put a man on the spot in Paris as a kind of Swedish ambassador for cultural affairs. The remarkable correspondence between Daniel Cronström (1655–1719) and Tessin between 1693 and 1718 (published in part as *Les Relations artistiques entre la France et la Suède*, Stockholm, 1964) documents the shaping of the collection and gives full details on the circumstances of a considerable number of the sheets shown in this exhibition. The most remarkable stories contained in these pages are certainly those relating to the drawings made by André Le Nôtre, Louis XIV's great garden architect, and to

the acquisition in 1702 of drawings of the silver used on the French king's table. No less interesting are the scattered references to hundreds of drawings acquired from Jean I Berain, Louis XIV's own designer of the chamber and *menus plaisirs* (also the principal stage designer of the period), and to the procurement of drawings by Nicolas de Launay (died 1727), possibly the leading silversmith of this time in France and a neglected major figure in the history of the decorative arts.

Carl Hårleman (1700–1753), a later royal architect in Sweden, is perhaps less widely known than he should be for his role in the formation of the Nationalmuseum collection of architectural material. Hårleman was sent by the crown on a study trip to Paris from 1721 to 1725. He worked with two members of the Académie Royale d'Architecture, Claude Desgots and Jacques Cazés, and gained access to the collection of drawings left by Le Nôtre to Desgots. Hårleman copied a number of these and also acquired a substantial number of French sheets during his study years and possibly on later trips to Paris. Since Hårleman inherited Tessin's collection and stamped it with his stamp, it is often rather difficult to determine the person responsible for the acquisition of a particular sheet in what is now called the Tessin-Hårleman Collection at the Nationalmuseum.

It may be argued that as the eighteenth century progressed, the Swedes' collecting of architectural and ornamental drawing was slightly out of phase with "modern" developments in France. Although Hårleman sought fashionable paintings by Jean-Baptiste Oudry (1686–1755) and François Boucher (1703–1770) for the Royal Palace and royal collections, and Carl Gustaf, Tessin the Younger's son, became a famous collector of master drawings by great painters, including contemporaries (these are now at the Nationalmuseum), a different approach was characteristic of architectural acquisitions, which continued to reflect a taste for the great achievements of Louis XIV's reign. This conservative attitude is evident in the drawings collected by Carl Johan Cronstedt (1707–1783), Hårleman's successor. Carl David Moselius (*Audran*, 1950) has written: "He threw himself with a particular ardor into the study of the architecture of the Splendid Century. His interest was first and foremost the royal châteaus and gardens: Versailles, Marly, Fontainebleau." At the height of the rococo in France, the achievements of Louis XIV's time were still much appreciated in Sweden.

Cronstedt was an avid collector. (He was not above pilfering the Swedish royal collections to add sheets to his own, which for many years remained in private hands.) His most important acquisition was that of the collection of Claude III Audran (1658–1734), consisting of some eighteen hundred sheets (see No. 12). This collection is of the greatest importance, since it contains nearly all of the remaining drawings of a lesser-known but significant French painter of Louis XIV's reign who was the teacher of Antoine Watteau. Moreover, only two other complete collections of the period survive, those of Charles Le Brun and of Pierre Mignard (1621–1695), both at the Louvre. The Cronstedt collection was acquired by the Nationalmuseum in 1942. Today, the Tessin-Hårleman and Cronstedt collections together contain about eighteen thousand sheets.

The Swedish collections of Versailles drawings are more important than any other group outside of France, and it should be remembered that with the exception of the Audran material, each of the Swedish sheets was carefully selected to represent some important aspect of French design that had not been adequately published. The French national collections are what survives of the entire output of the royal workshop, unedited. At Stockholm, however, we have the selections of highly trained design professionals, and, thus, an informed assessment of important French achievements. The Stockholm drawings by Le Nôtre, Ballin, and Berain rival anything to be found in France, and the collections of drawings by Nicolas-Amboise Cousinet and Nicolas de Launay of French silver are perhaps more important than any that remain in Paris. Altogether, the Swedish holdings of French drawings of architecture and the decorative arts are broad in scope, including subjects not only from Versailles, but from many other châteaus, gardens, and significant buildings in France, as well.

Selections from the Nationalmuseum collection have been shown in a series of exhibitions in Paris and Stockholm over a period of years. In 1985 nearly all of the drawings from the Nationalmuseum relating to Versailles and a small group of drawings evoking the nearby royal châteaus of Trianon, Marly, and Clagny were shown at the Centre Culturel Suédois in Paris. The exhibition, entitled *Versailles à Stockholm*, formed the basis of *Versailles: The View from Sweden*, which is the first showing of this material in the United States.

Guy Walton
New York University

Catalogue

Per Bjurström	P.B.
Agneta Börtz-Laine	A.B.-L.
Elaine Evans Dee	E.E.D.
Börje Magnusson	B.M.
Astrid Tydén-Jordan	A.T.-J.
Guy Walton	G.W.
Tessin-Hårleman Collection	THC
Cronstedt Collection	CC

Frequently Cited Titles

Audran, 1950 — *Claude Audran, L'Art décoratif français au Musée de Stockholm.* Paris, Bibliothèque Nationale, 1950.

B.S.H.A.F. — *Bulletin de la Société de l'histoire de l'art français.*

de La Gorce, 1986 — Jérôme de La Gorce, *Berain: Dessinateur du roi soleil.* Paris, 1986.

Hernmarck, 1953 — Carl Hernmarck, "Claude Ballin et quelques dessins de pièces d'argenterie du Musée National de Stockholm." *Gazette des Beaux-Arts* 41 (1953): 103–18, 137–40.

Hernmarck, 1977 — Carl Hernmarck, *The Art of the European Silversmith.* 2 vols. London, 1977.

Josephson, 1930 — Ragnar Josephson, *Nicodème Tessin à la cour de Louis XIV.* Paris and Brussels, 1930.

Josephson, 1938 — Ragnar Josephson, *Tessin.* 2 vols. Stockholm, 1938–39.

Kommer, 1974 — Björn R. Kommer, *Nicodemus Tessin der Jungere und das Stockholmer Schloss.* Heidelberg, 1974.

Le Brun, 1963 — *Charles Lebrun, 1619–1690, peintre et dessinateur.* Versailles, 1963.

A. Marie, 1968 — Alfred Marie, *Naissance de Versailles.* 2 vols. Paris, 1968.

A. and J. Marie, 1972 — Alfred Marie and Jeanne Marie, *Mansart à Versailles.* 2 vols. Paris, 1972.

A. and J. Marie, 1976 — Alfred Marie and Jeanne Marie, *Versailles au temps de Louis XIV.* Paris, 1976.

Paris, 1951 — *Versailles et les châteaux de France, trois cents dessins du Musée National de Stockholm.* Paris and Versailles, 1951.

Paris, 1985 — *Versailles à Stockholm.* Paris, Institut Culturel Suédois, 1985.

S.S.H. — *Stockholm Slotts Historia.* 3 vols. Stockholm, 1940–41.

Stockholm, 1942 — *Arkitekturritninger, planer och teckninger ur Carl Johan Cronstedts.* Stockholm, Nationalmuseum, 1942.

Stockholm, 1978 — *Nicodemus Tessin D. Y.* Stockholm, Tessinska Palatset, 1978.

Stockholm, 1986 — *Kung Sol i Sverige.* Stockholm, Nationalmuseum, 1986.

Thornton, 1978 — Peter Thornton, *Seventeenth-Century Interior Decoration in England, France and Holland.* New Haven and London, 1978.

Thornton, 1984 — Peter Thornton, *Authentic Decor.* London, 1984.

Tydén-Jordan, 1985 — Astrid Tydén-Jordan, *Kröningsvagen-Konstverk och riksklenod.* Stockholm, 1985.

Walton, 1986 — Guy Walton, *Louis XIV's Versailles.* Chicago, 1986.

Weigert, 1931 — R.-A. Weigert, "Recherches sur quelques dessins de la vaiselle du Grand roi." *Revue de l'histoire de Versailles*, 1931, pp. 206–21.

Weigert and Hernmarck, 1964 — R.-A. Weigert and Carl Hernmarck, *Les Relations artistiques entre la France et la Suède 1693–1718.* Stockholm, 1964.

1.
Unknown Draftsman
France, 1687
Versailles: Large Plan of the Château, Town, Gardens, and Surroundings
Pen and black and red ink, black chalk, gray, green, and blue wash;
    126 × 57 cm.
Inscribed throughout
Bibliography: R. Strandberg, "André Le Nôtre et son école,"
    B.S.H.A.F., 1960, p. 123; Paris, 1985, no. A4; Stockholm, 1986,
    no. 7
Nationalmuseum, Stockholm, THC 1

Details of this plan allow it to be precisely dated to 1687, a great moment in the history of Versailles. The château was then reaching its full dimensions, and the principal outbuildings such as the stables, commons (the lodging and eating place for much of the permanent staff), and the first architect Jules Hardouin-Mansart's (1646–1708) great Orangerie were all completed and in use. The gardens were also at their most spectacular, reflecting the great achievement of the decade: the successful bringing of water to Versailles to allow the playing of the many fountains for a number of hours each day. The Grand Trianon was under rapid construction; in just nine months it went from the planning stage to the setting for one of the king's dinners.

The date also coincides perfectly with the visit to Versailles of Nicodemus Tessin the Younger (1654–1728), the superintendent of buildings for the Swedish king. In all probability this sheet was commissioned by Tessin to take home with him along with his notes and diaries.

This era of great works came rapidly to a halt two years later during the War of the League of Augsburg (1688–97). In 1685 Louis XIV had spent 11,300,000 livres on works for Versailles; in 1689 the amount was only 1,710,000 livres; and in 1690 work nearly stopped, as may be deduced from the sum of 368,000 livres spent that year.
G.W.

2.
André Le Nôtre (1613–1700)
France
Versailles: The Parterre d'Amour
Pen and black ink, blue and gray wash; 43.6 × 28.5 cm.
Inscribed: *Executé à versaille par Monsr. Le Noster/le 6e Mars Lan 1682*;
    scale in *toises*
Bibliography: A. Marie, 1968, I, p. 29, pl. IX; Paris, 1985, no. B1;
    Stockholm, 1986, no. 8
Nationalmuseum, Stockholm, THC 7774

The principal interest of this drawing is its inscription, which identifies it as the work of André Le Nôtre, Louis XIV's gardener and, arguably, the greatest garden designer of all time. Le Nôtre was from a family of gardeners and was raised in the Tuileries gardens in Paris. His first masterpiece, executed in 1656, when he was already forty-three years old, was the garden of the Château de Vaux-le-Vicomte for Nicolas Fouquet, the minister of finance. He was immediately employed by Louis XIV for the gardens of Fontainebleau, but his most famous work was the park at Versailles, the scheme of which evolved piece by piece after 1662 over more than a decade.

Though the sheet shows only the detail of four flower beds and nine fountains arranged within a rectangular shape, such

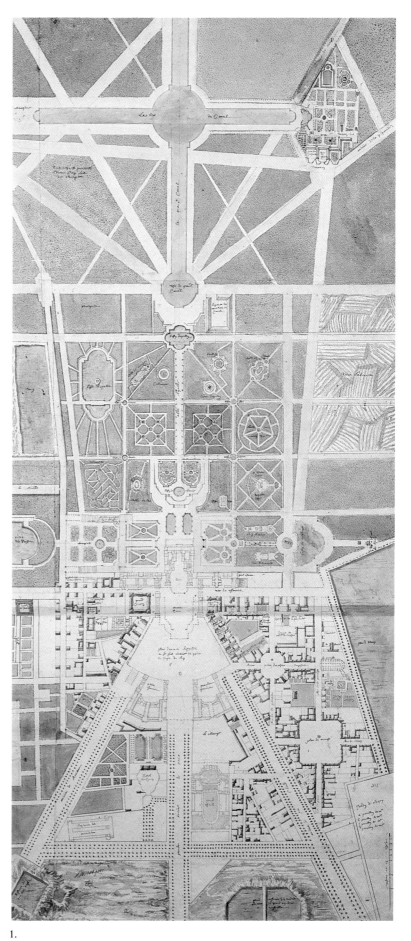

1.

ornamental studies, modeled on embroidery patterns, were seen by seventeenth-century connoisseurs of garden design as particularly choice examples of one of the more refined aspects of garden planning.

Le Nôtre's autograph drawings are extremely rare, and the historical details of place and date of design in the inscription on this sheet are unique. The inscription makes it clear that this is not a working drawing. It was possibly done as a souvenir for a visitor or to stimulate discussion for changes in these beds.

G.W.

2.

3.
André Le Nôtre (1613–1700)
France
Versailles: Project for a Giant Cascade
Pen and black ink, red chalk, blue and gray wash; 41.8 × 32 cm.
Inscribed on verso: *vue St. Denis pres la porte devant l'hotel de St. Chaumont M. Lambert*
Bibliography: Paris, 1951, no. 208; R. Strandberg, "André Le Nôtre et son école," *B.S.H.A.F.*, 1960, p. 23; Gerold Weber, "Ein Kaskadenprojekt für Versailles . . . ," *Zeitschrift für Kunstgeschichte*, 1974, p. 258, fig. 9; Paris, 1985, no. B25; Stockholm, 1986, no. 9
Nationalmuseum, Stockholm, THC 7811

With much of the great new water-gathering system for Versailles nearly completed, a truly extravagant new fountain seemed an appropriate addition to the park in the mid-1680s. Gerold Weber has traced the complicated history of a series of projects drawn up between 1684 and 1687 for the area in the trees to the north of the Latona parterre. Weber points out that Le Nôtre included a significant number of sculptures in his work. In 1687 Jean-Baptiste Tuby (1635–1700) signed and dated a clay model (now in the Los Angeles County Museum of Art) for the central reclining Venus group shown in the drawing.

The drawing itself is consistent with what is known of Le Nôtre's working style. At one time, so little importance was assigned to this sheet that it was annotated, presumably by the Lambert of the inscription (probably the architect listed in 1699 as a member of the Académie Royale d'Architecture) and used as a folder.

G.W.

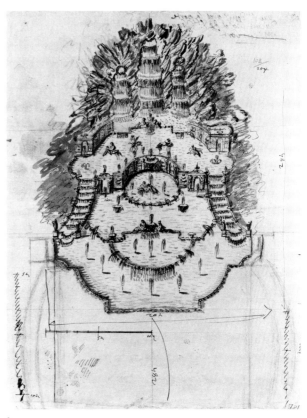

4.
School of Charles Le Brun (1619–1690)
France
Fountain
Pen and black ink, brown, yellow, and gray wash; 58.2 × 48.8 cm.
Inscribed: *C. Le Brun invenit en l'an 1673*
Bibliography: Paris, 1951, no. 76; G. Weber, "Charles Le Brun's 'Recueil de divers dessins de fontaines,' " *Münchner Jahrbuch*, 1981, pp. 151–81; Paris, 1985, no. B11
Nationalmuseum, Stockholm, CC 146

The subject of this drawing is reminiscent of the Pyramid Fountain of François Girardon (1628–1715) in the parterre below the king's State Apartment at Versailles. Through the inclusion of the arms of France and female allegories of Abundance with symbols of War and Peace, it also resembles a sculptural group still present in the triumphal arch bosquet in the trees north of the château.

3.

4.

Gerold Weber, comparing the sheet to the book *Recueil de divers dessins de fontaines*, by Charles Le Brun, Louis XIV's premier painter, finds that it represents that artist's taste in garden-fountain design. This is a good example of Le Brun's fountain style rarely realized at Versailles. There, most plans for ornamentation of the gardens were the result of collaboration among the king, his ministers, his gardeners, and his architects, with no individual responsible for the rather detailed designs that were handed over to the sculptors. Until his fall from favor in the 1680s, Charles Le Brun was certainly the most influential figure in the arts during the reign of Louis XIV. He not only worked as a painter, but also supplied designs for tapestries, furniture, and sculptures. The most successful period of his career at Versailles began with his designs for the figures and reliefs for the palace exterior (1670–73) and for twenty-eight marble groups, to be placed in front of the center section of the château's garden façade around a clover-shaped basin but now dispersed in the gardens and elsewhere. It culminated in the creation of the program and design of the ceiling of the Hall of Mirrors (1678–84). This drawing, although it may not be autograph, is an example of Le Brun's ornamental and figurative style, which combined French classicism with elements of the Italian baroque.

G.W.

5.
Workshop of Jules Hardouin-Mansart (1646–1708)
France
Versailles: Plan and Elevation of the Colonnade
Pen and black ink, gray, blue, yellow, and green wash; 37.4 × 24 cm.
Inscribed: *plan et elevation de la colonnade / dans des bosquest de Versailles*
Bibliography: Paris, 1985, no. B24; Walton, 1986, fig. 98
Nationalmuseum, Stockholm, THC 9

In 1687 Tessin wrote in his journal from Paris: "The Colonnade, all made of marble, is the latest piece [in the park of Versailles] and is not quite completed; there are 52 columns of different colors with Ionic orders of the capitals and bases of white marble with little imposts above which are very unattractive. . . . There are arcades running all around, between the arches there are triangular bas-reliefs of marble; between the columns there are great vases of white marble 13 *qu.* wide from which jets of water shoot everywhere. . . . Most of the reliefs and vases are not yet in place. . . . There is a small water channel which runs along the columns all way round." The project shown in this drawing, which illustrates one quarter of the structure, is not identical to that described by Tessin, and is clearly an early idea.

The Colonnade, which still stands, represents a very important transition in the history of the Versailles gardens. It was the first major element designed by the architect Jules Hardouin-Mansart rather than Le Nôtre, the gardener. Le Nôtre, prodded by the king to express an opinion, had the following comment, as recorded in the memoirs of the duc de Saint-Simon: "You have used an architect and he has given you one of the tricks of his trade." This is a rare instance of a public disagreement between those who worked for the king, and it reflects a turning point when the aged gardener was being pushed toward retirement and the influence of the royal architect was being extended.

plan de Elévation de la Colonnade
de 3 des Bosquets de Versailles.

Bosquets

Salle

Echelle de cinq toises   Planche N°9.

5.

6.

Robert Berger has noted that the stone used was deliberately selected to show the beauty of the products of the French quarries (*In the Garden of the Sun King*, Washington, D.C., 1985, pp. 41–49).

G.W.

6.
Workshop of Louis Le Vau (1612–1700)
France
Versailles: Project for an Enveloppe *Palace*
Pen and black ink, gray, blue and red wash; 16.8 × 79 cm.
Bibliography: Paris, 1951, no. 5; A. Marie, 1968, II, p. 227, pl. CVII; Thomas Hall, *Arkitekturritningar och gravyr ur Nationalmuseums Samlingar*, Versailles and Stockholm, 1974, p. 18; Jean-Claude Le Guillou, "Aperçu sur un projet insolite (1668) pour le Château de Versailles," *Gazette des Beaux-Arts* 95 (1980): 52, fig. 3; Robert W. Berger, *Versailles: The Château of Louis XIV*, University Park, Pa., 1985, pp. 23–26, fig. 13; Paris, 1985, no. C1

Louis Le Vau, the architect, along with Charles Le Brun and André Le Nôtre, was one of the triumvirate that during the 1660s transformed the small red-brick hunting lodge of Louis XIII into Louis XIV's great palace. This drawing dates from 1668, according to J.-C. Le Guillou and Robert Berger, and shows an early, otherwise unknown phase of Louis XIV's project to create a château worthy of the stupendous garden Le Nôtre was completing.

Jean-Baptiste Colbert, the royal superintendent of buildings, coined the phrase "the envelope project" to describe a plan in which the old château would be preserved while enclosed on the garden side by a nobler building. In this drawing a giant order (seen on the right) joins the upper and middle floors of an Italianate palace.

This sheet also shows proposals for additions to the château on the town, or eastern, side. The central part of the drawing is a careful record of the appearance of the Louis XIII château as embellished by Louis XIV during the 1660s. The building is well known from a bird's-eye view painted by Pierre I Patel (1605–1676) in 1668, now in the Musée National du Château de Versailles.

At the end of that year, in a description of a great garden fête, Mlle de Scudéry wrote that soon all was about to change at Versailles and, referring to the new *enveloppe* palace, that in a year's time the place would be unrecognizable.

G.W.

7.
Workshop of François d'Orbay? (1634–1697)
France
Versailles: Louis XIV's Bathroom and Adjoining Bedroom
Pen and black ink, black, red, and green wash; 39.7 × 41.5 cm.
Inscribed on verso: *Pour les bains; marbres (?) des deux pieces d'anbas a mesure*
Bibliography: Stockholm, 1942, no. 41, Paris, 1951, no. 11; Albert Laprade, *François d'Orbay*, Paris, 1960, pl. VII-3; A. Marie, 1968, II, pl. CXVII; Paris, 1985, C4; Walton, 1986, fig. 113
Nationalmuseum, Stockholm, CC 397

When Le Vau's *enveloppe* palace was built, the definition of the interior areas remained under discussion. On the north and northwest sides, however, a series of rooms on the ground floor was luxuriously fitted out for the king. This was

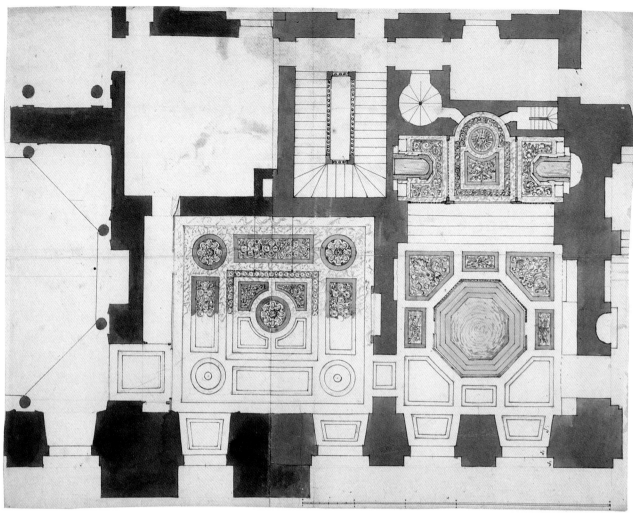

7.

8.

the Lower Apartment of His Majesty destined for social events. (Louis slept upstairs.) Immediately adjoining these rooms, facing west, was the Apartment of the Baths.

This drawing shows the arrangement of the walls and the projects for the decoration of the floors of the bathroom itself and of the adjoining bedroom, for resting after bathing. These rooms were completed, but today only a few window shutters showing marine subjects from the baths survive at the château, while the central basin from the bath has been reemployed as a fountain at the entry of the Orangerie. Louis's decision to build a bath may owe something to his mother's preferences. Ann of Austria had a famous bath at the Palais Royale decorated by well-known painters. It was one of the sights of Paris in the 1650s. While Ann was known as being exceptionally conscious of hygiene, her son never had that reputation. Louis's three tubs suggest that his baths may have been taken for the sensual pleasure they afforded; possibly the bathwaters were of different temperatures or scents. The bathroom had running water and was warmed by a heating system related to the hot-water tanks. The large central pool may have been a decorative fountain. The drawing also shows an unrealized plan for an octagonal salon (center left) and a tub arrangement (upper right) that was not used.

Versailles at this time was being transformed into a splendid setting for the daily life of the king. The court was present at Louis's rising and retiring, and this plan suggests that the ritual of a royal bath also must have been luxurious. G.W.

8.
François d'Orbay (1634–1697)
France
Versailles: Vestibule Wall Decoration
Pen and black and brown ink, red chalk, gray wash; 24.7 × 53 cm.
Verso: red chalk drawing of an octagonal structure
Bibliography: Paris, 1951, no. 26; Albert Laprade, *François d'Orbay*, Paris, 1960, pl. VII-6A; A. Marie, 1968, II, pl. CXXVI; Paris, 1985, no. C7; Stockholm, 1986, no. 12
Nationalmuseum, Stockholm, CC 2978

From 1670 to 1671, a grand staircase was planned at the east end of the king's apartments at Versailles. The vestibule shown in this drawing was behind the stairway and opened on the west onto the Lower Apartment of His Majesty, and north onto the gardens. The decoration was executed in painted plaster, brightly colored in red and gold to resemble marble and gilt. Some fragments of the paintings, extensively restored, survive on the walls.

The decoration of a vestibule differed from that of other rooms at the time in its architectural character, meant to simulate masonry decoration with sculptural ornaments. The statues, probably representing Mars, the god of war, and Minerva, the goddess of wisdom, evoke the mythological themes that dominated the decor of the whole château at the time.

Albert Laprade identifies the author of this sheet as François d'Orbay, who during the 1670s was royal architect and chief of the royal workshop of draftsmen. After the death of Le Vau in 1670, no new first architect was appointed to design the remaining elements of the *enveloppe* palace. Although

Laprade assigns most of this work to d'Orbay, in all probability there were a number of artists involved, not all architects, including Charles Le Brun.
G.W.

9.
François d'Orbay? (1634–1697)
France
Versailles: End of the South Wing
Pen and black ink, black chalk, gray wash; 32 × 21.7 cm.
Bibliography: Paris, 1951, no. 6; Paris, 1985, no. C16; Stockholm, 1986, no. 10
Nationalmuseum, Stockholm, CC 1454

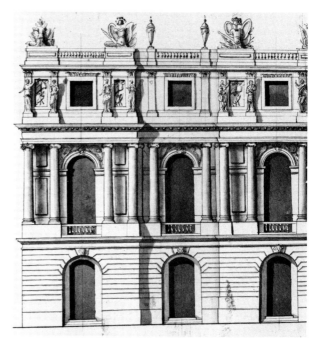

9.

In 1677 or 1678 Jules Hardouin-Mansart, the royal architect, proposed a number of solutions to the need for more space at Versailles. Several projects are known from drawings, and most suggested the addition of one or more floors to the *enveloppe* palace. One of these plans at the Archives Nationales shows little change in the central part of the château beyond the suppression of the terrace and its replacement by a gallery (eventually the Hall of Mirrors), and the creation of an impressive adjoining salon. That sheet probably indicates a decision to build laterally, leaving the central portion of the new château largely unchanged. Additional drawings indicate that at one point separate wings to the north and south of the *enveloppe* were planned; finally, however, an attached south wing was begun. Mansart's design of its exterior, shown in this drawing, reflected the elevation of the *enveloppe* palace, along with changes in the fenestration necessitated by the lighting problems of the Hall of Mirrors. This drawing suggests Mansart's new scheme.

The south wing (Aisle du Midi), which was built primarily to house the growing family of Louis XIV, contained a number of splendid interiors. These lodgings were so grand that important social events occasionally took place there.

The drawing is close to the style associated with d'Orbay. His authorship may be questioned on the basis of the clear origin of the plan in Mansart's studio. If, however, d'Orbay is seen as working in the capacity of first royal draftsman rather than as an independent architect, the attribution might be sustained. D'Orbay moved from Versailles to Chambord about this time, so if this is his work for Versailles, it must be one of his last.
G.W.

10.
Royal Workshops
France, 1671
Versailles: Project for the Ceiling, Cabinet of Monsieur
Pen and black ink, gray wash; 29.7 × 28 cm.
Inscribed: *Plafond pour le cabinet de Monsieur /a Versailles*; on verso: *No 4* and a cypher
Bibliography: Paris, 1951, no. 9; A. Marie, 1968, II, pl. CXXVIII, Paris, 1985, no. C8
Nationalmuseum, Stockholm, THC 8727

"Monsieur," in the language of the court, was Philippe d'Orléans, Louis XIV's only sibling. He was second or third in line to the throne for many years. His own splendid château, with decorations that rivaled the king's houses, was near Versailles

10.

at Saint-Cloud. Nonetheless, he was assigned an apartment in the same area as the Dauphin, Louis's only legitimate son and heir, on the ground floor of the south side of the *enveloppe* palace directly under the apartment of the queen.

Four drawings, two at the Nationalmuseum, Stockholm, and two in the Bibliothèque Nationale, Paris, remain for the ceiling of this apartment. The alternative to this drawing was selected and is in the Bibliothèque Nationale (Estampes, Va 361 IV).

This is a fine example of the kind of plaster ceiling, generally executed by Italian craftsmen, that became extremely popular in France and throughout Europe at the time. The ceiling in the drawing contains an illusionistic central panel, which was certainly intended to be painted. The apparent preference for figural paintings set in deep plaster frames may account for the rejection of this design.

G.W.

11.
Royal Workshops
France, 1671
Versailles: Project for the Ceiling of the Bedroom and Bed Alcove of Monsieur
Pen and black ink, gray wash; 29.8 × 39 cm.
Inscribed: *Plafond pour la chambre de lapartment de Monsieur / A versailles / Le Roy a choisy ce dessin/Plafond de lalcove.*
Bibliography: Paris, 1951, no. 10; A. Marie, 1968, II, pl. CXXIX; Paris, 1985, no. C9; Stockholm, 1986, no. 13
Nationalmuseum, Stockholm, THC 8754

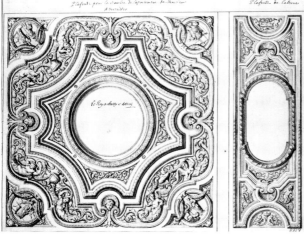

11.

Shortly after he began to rule alone, Louis XIV ordered that all projects for buildings were to be studied by himself and that two projects were always to be submitted so that a choice could be made. Presumably, for important works his minister, Jean-Baptiste Colbert, or the artist made a presentation speech explaining the features of each project. Many such highly finished drawings have inscriptions indicating acceptance or rejection by the king and/or Colbert. According to the inscription, this design was selected.

The division of the ceiling decoration shown in the drawing differentiates the bed area from the rest of the room. The king's own bedchamber had a balustrade at the foot of the bed, and the floor by the bed was often made of inlaid wood in elaborate patterns. Something of this grandeur must have been found in the king's brother's room.

G.W.

12.
Claude III Audran (1658–1734)
France
Versailles: Ceiling of the Private Bedroom of the Princesse de Conti in the South Wing
Watercolor; 23.1 × 34.4 cm.
Inscribed: *petite Chambre à coucher de S.A.S. Madame la princesse de Conty*; scale
Bibliography: *Audran*, 1950, no. 7; A. and J. Marie, 1972, I, fig. p. 249; Paris, 1985, no. C22; Stockholm, 1986, no. 14
Nationalmuseum, Stockholm, CC II, 36

On August 10, 1734, the Swedish royal architect Carl Johan Cronstedt (1707–1783) wrote from Paris to his mother in Sweden: "I'm in the process of negotiating for an inheritance. This is the purchase of a large number of drawings left

12.

by one Audran who made them during his whole life." Audran was, in fact, a figure of international importance, and Tessin had even attempted to lure him to Stockholm without success. He was a great decorator who, like Jean I Berain (1640–1711), used delicate grotesque motifs. Though Audran usually worked at the fringe of Louis XIV's court—for example, at Meudon for the Dauphin—he did decorate the famous rooms in the Versailles Zoo for Louis XIV's favorite, his granddaughter-in-law, the duchess of Burgundy (see No. 20). He was also employed by the princesse de Conti, the king's daughter by his mistress Mme de Montespan, to decorate two rooms of her Versailles apartment. The ceiling shown here was for a small room for personal use.

This fine example of Audran's draftsmanship is one of the very few that are inscribed, and it therefore may be associated with a specific project.
G.W.

13.
Unknown Draftsman
France, 1680s
Versailles: Embroidered Wall Hanging for the Throne Room
Pen and black ink, watercolor; 66.7 × 49.1 cm.
Inscribed: *Meuble brodée dans la Sale d'Audience de l'Apartement a Versailles*
Bibliography: R. A. Weigert, "Le meuble brodé de la salle du trône du grand roi à Versailles," *Revue de l'art ancien et moderne*, Paris, 1932, II, pp. 97–108; Paris, 1985, no. C13; Stockholm, 1986, no. 17; Walton, 1986, fig. 21
Nationalmuseum, Stockholm, THC 1554

In fact, Versailles had no throne room, though such a room existed at the Tuileries Palace in Paris. The inscription shows that its author was sensitive to this point, since it refers to the Audience Room. That room was on the second floor of the château in the Grand Apartment of the King. The room had originally been designated as the king's state bedroom, and its ceiling had been decorated with Apollo crossing the sky in his chariot—the solar climactic scene of a series of rooms showing the planets in mythological guise.

When the king chose to sleep elsewhere and to use the Grand Apartment for official purposes, it was decided to install the eight-foot-high solid-silver throne, complemented with a number of other large pieces of solid-silver furniture, in this room. Louis rarely sat on the throne and on social occasions often sat on the steps leading up to it to watch the dancing that, surprisingly, took place here. Tessin described the wall hanging: "The hanging (*meuble*) is distinguished by pilasters embroidered in thick gold relief an inch deep. The figures are almost life-sized and the bare skin is rendered with silver thread. The rest is embroidered in gold sometimes four or five inches deep, most especially in the trophies shown below. Some colors have been mixed in for accent throughout to make the design easier to read. The background is all in embroidered silver."

This and other hangings were alternatively hung on the wall when four paintings by Guido Reni of the Labors of Hercules and other canvases were not on view. The hangings may have been a gift to the king from Mme de Montespan, since she was a famous patron of the great embroidery workshops of the Convent of Saint-Joseph in Paris.
G.W.

Meuble Brodée dans la Sale d'Audience de l'Apartement a Versailles.

1554.

13.

A a S.t Jean de raphaele   B a Jame du dominiquin

14.

15.

14.
Unknown Draftsman
France, after 1701
Versailles: Louis XIV's Bedroom
Black chalk, watercolor; 20.5 × 31.9 cm.
Inscribed: *A le St Jean de raphaele; B le david du dominiquin*
Bibliography: Stockholm, 1942, no. 45; Paris, 1951, no. 29; François Souchal, *French Sculptors, Reign of Louis XIV*, London, 1977, I, p. 161; Paris, 1985, no. C24; Stockholm, 1986, no. 15; Walton, 1986, fig. 6
Nationalmuseum, Stockholm, CC 174

Only a handful of drawings of the interior of Versailles from the time of Louis XIV survive. This example is a careful rendering that documents the placement of the furniture and, in the inscription, identifies the pictures on either side of the bed as the work of Raphael and of Domenichino.

In 1701, Louis moved his bedroom to the center area of the west side of the Marble Court, near the center of the château. This change has often been seen as a gesture charged with symbolic meaning, since the king's rising and retiring before his full court were major ritual events in the life of the château. Equally important was the fact that the room was built at precisely the time France entered a difficult war against the rest of Europe over the Spanish succession. This redecoration may be seen as an act of bravado on the king's part to suggest that the life and art of Versailles would be left undisturbed by the war.

The monumentally cold and grand decoration favored earlier in the reign was here replaced with more graceful and delicate ornament, and the interior gained a special lightness by the exclusive use of white paint and gilt. The walls and overdoors were hung with important works of art proclaiming the high artistic standard typical of the royal collection.
G.W.

15.
Unknown Draftsman
France, after 1701
Versailles: Northwest Corner of Louis XIV's Bedroom
Pen and brown ink, black chalk, watercolor; 23.3 × 18.2 cm.
Inscribed on lining: *Raphaelle*
Bibliography: Stockholm, 1942, no. 46; Paris, 1951, no. 30; Paris, 1985, no. C25; Stockholm, 1986, no. 16
Nationalmuseum, Stockholm, CC 513

Although this view of the bedroom was drawn after 1701 as was No. 14, the tapestries and pictures on the walls are different. This discrepancy may reflect the alteration of the decoration for the change of season, or perhaps the drawing represents the appearance of the room after Louis XIV's death. By tradition, the furnishings of the king's bedroom were left at his death to the first gentleman of the bedchamber.

The tapestry covering the doorway behind the bed rail shown in the drawing was made after cartoons by Claude III Audran.
G.W.

16.
Royal Workshops
France, probably 1688
Versailles: Section of the Chapel
Pen and black ink, green, blue, red, and gray wash; 43.3 × 71.5 cm.
Bibliography: Paris, 1951, no. 48; Michael Petzet, "Quelques Projets
 inédits pour la Chapelle de Versailles," *Art de France* 1 (1961): 317;
 Paris, 1985, no. D8; Walton, 1986, fig. 137
Nationalmuseum, Stockholm, THC 8067

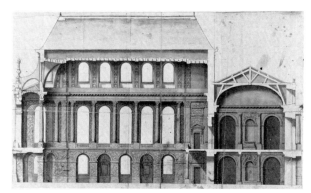

16.

When Tessin was in France in 1687, the major new project under consideration for Versailles was the palace chapel. (The court was using a temporary building from 1681). In 1684, it had seemed that the issue was settled. A large domed church had been planned in connection with the building of a new north wing, symmetrical with the south wing. In an unusual departure from the practice of the king's buildings office, Jean Le Blond had published five or six designs for this project, but in 1688 that original scheme was abandoned. The marquis de Dangeau remarked in his journal that Louis XIV had decided to build a *sainte-chapelle* (that is to say, a building resembling the famous Gothic church in Paris). The foundations of the new Versailles church were laid down in 1689, but work stopped after a short time because of the financial crisis caused by military expenditures. Work resumed on the chapel when Jules Hardouin-Mansart assumed the superintendency of the king's buildings office in 1699; the chapel was inaugurated in 1710.

This important drawing shows the south side of the chapel's interior invested with marble. It must have been made before the royal decision was reached on December 22, 1698, to use white stone. The sheet might date from 1688 or from a second phase begun in 1698.

The Versailles chapel is one of the most original works done by the royal workshops. In an age when classical standards dominated architectural thinking, the combination of a Gothic ground plan and soaring interior space with a carefully studied Corinthian order in the Greco-Roman tradition was unprecedented. The chapel may be seen as brilliantly integrating elements taken from the aesthetic of medieval building into the canon of classical architecture. The combination of styles used at Versailles was undoubtedly an attempt to suggest the special relationship of the French church to royal ecclesiastical traditions of the Middle Ages.
G.W.

17.
Royal Workshops
France, c. 1688
Versailles: North Elevation of the Chapel
Pen and black ink, gray, green, blue and red wash; 71.5 × 43.3 cm.
Bibliography: Paris, 1951, no. 46; Michael Petzet, "Quelques projets
 inédits pour la Chapelle de Versailles," *Art en France* 1 (1961): 317;
 Paris, 1985, no. D10
Nationalmuseum, Stockholm, THC 8062

This and the roughly contemporary previous sheet, along with others at Stockholm, testify to Tessin's intense interest in the Versailles chapel, which he did not know firsthand.
G.W.

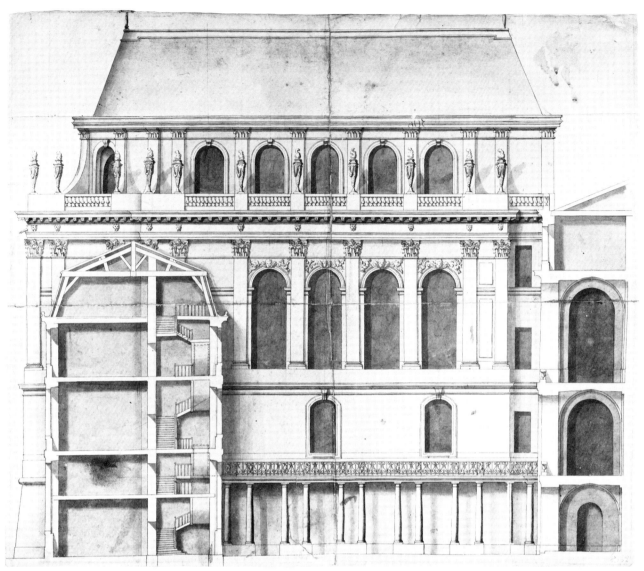

17.

18.

19.

18.
René Charpentier (1680–1723)
France
Versailles: Trophy Relief for the Chapel
Pen and black ink, gray and rose wash; 40.9 × 10.5 cm.
Inscribed: *fait charp . . . / Charpentier*
Bibliography: Paris, 1951, no. 55; François Souchal, *French Sculptors, Reign of Louis XIV*, London, 1977, I, p. 87, no. 3; Paris, 1985, no. D13; Bruno Pons, *De Paris à Versailles*, Strasbourg, 1986, pp. 40–41
Nationalmuseum, Stockholm, THC 2145

About 1708, at a political and financial low point in the history of Louis XIV's reign, the unexpected decision was made to proceed with the elaborate decoration of the interior of the chapel. Vast ceiling paintings were commissioned from Antoine Coypel, Jean Jouvenet, and Charles de Lafosse, along with an extensive program of relief sculpture, including both figures and ornament, to cover most of the stone surfaces of the interior. The highly original ornament is the harbinger of the rococo style, as Fiske Kimball perceptively observes in his *Creation of the Rococo* (Philadephia, 1943, p. 82). The decor marks an important departure from the norms of decoration of Louis XIV's reign.

The trophy motif was hardly original and had figured in the ornamental decorations at Versailles from the beginning. Two features distinguish the chapel reliefs: the ingenious use of ecclesiastical elements (as opposed to arms) and the use of floral elements and ribbons. The subject depicted in the center of this relief is described by François Souchal as Religion, holding in her hand a cross and a Bible, crushing Heresy with her foot.

Bruno Pons attributes this drawing to René Charpentier on the basis of the inscription and its resemblance to other of his works. The sculptor, one of many who worked at the chapel, was paid 500 livres for the execution of this relief, which occupies the north side of the fifth pillar on the left of the chapel.
G.W.

19.
René Charpentier (1680–1723)
France
Versailles: Trophy Relief for the Chapel
Pen and black ink, gray and rose wash; 46 × 14.3 cm.
Inscribed: *Charpentier*
Bibliography: Paris, 1951, no. 57; Paris, 1985, no. D14
Nationalmuseum, Stockholm, THC 1008

This trophy decorates the west side of the second pillar on the right of the chapel. A varied assortment of arms and ecclesiastical accessories surrounds an oval portrait of Christ.
G.W.

20.
Claude III Audran (1658–1734)
France
Ceiling, possibly for the Versailles Zoo
Red chalk, watercolor, gold paint; 33.8 × 29.4 cm.
Bibliography: *Audran*, 1950, no. 24; Paris, 1985, no. I4
Nationalmuseum, Stockholm, CC II 34

The presence of birds and animals in this drawing suggests it is a design for the ceiling of the zoo. Audran executed

20.

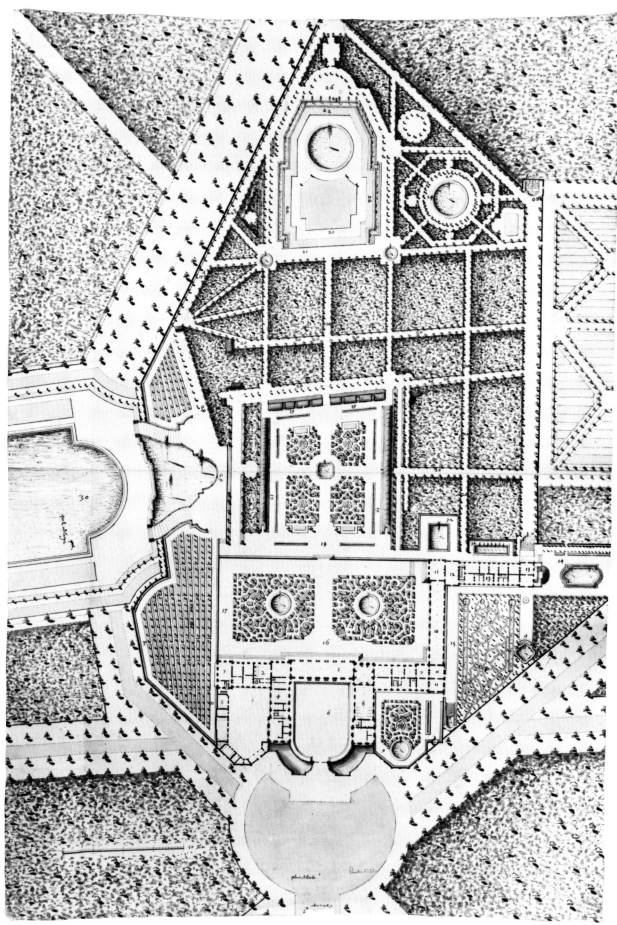

21.

paintings for the building and in 1700 was paid 27,800 livres for them, but there is nothing to confirm that this sheet actually pertains to that project. The drawing exhibits the pleasant, amusing delicacy characteristic of decorations made at the end of Louis XIV's reign. It was in the margin of a proposed program for the zoo, built for the king's grand-daughter-in-law, that Louis wrote his famous remark *il faut de la jeunesse*.

The zoo at Versailles was a small château surrounded by radiating enclosures for the collection of animals and large birds. It was possible to dine in an octagonal salon while looking out at the animals. It was one of the first major buildings in the Versailles park ready for the fêtes of the 1660s.

G.W.

21.
André Le Nôtre (1613–1700)
France
Versailles: Plan of the Grand Trianon
Pen and black ink, gray, green, blue, and brown wash; 96.5 × 66 cm.
Inscribed throughout; on verso: *Trianon*
Bibliography: Ragnar Josephson, "Le Grand Trianon sous Louis XIV," *Revue de l'histoire de Versailles*, 1927, pp. 1–24; P. Bourget, *J. H. Mansart*, Paris, 1960, fig. XLVII; A. and J. Marie, 1976, pp. 145–85; F. Hamilton Hazlehurst, *Gardens of Illusion: The Genius of André Le Nostre*, Nashville, 1980, p. 159, fig. 118; Paris, 1985, no. H1
Nationalmuseum, Stockholm, THC 22

Tessin was on hand for at least the beginning of one of the most fabulous exploits of the king's buildings office at Versailles. Within nine months in 1687, the old Trianon de Porcelaine was demolished and the Grand Trianon completed—all done without the first architect, who was absent taking a cure. "I went a few times to Trianon with M. Le Nôtre . . .," wrote Tessin. "There is a good chance that nothing made there will be worth anything." The Swedish architect must have been surprised when, back in Stockholm, he learned that the building as finished was regarded as successful. Tessin's curiosity led him to ask his representative in Paris to send him information in 1694. Daniel Cronström wrote: "I spoke to Monsieur Le Nostre. . . . He asked me to assure you that he will have a measured plan of the new Trianon made for you" (Weigert and Hernmarck, 1964, pp. 47–48). On September 26 Tessin wrote that the work and accompanying documents had reached him. This is the most fully documented drawing by the great Le Nôtre. In a memorandum the gardener remarked that he had taken a lot of trouble with it: "This description [of Trianon] with the largest plan that comes with it are by the hand of M. Le Nostre."

The arrangement of the palace shown here is that which followed the remodeling of 1692. Le Nôtre's remarks stress the relationship of the interior to the exterior of the building and the importance of a garden called The Springs, a creation that anticipates the naturalistic traditions of English gardens of the next century.

Trianon was a garden palace, a place for the particular appreciation of flowers. The king rarely slept there until a third bedroom was built for him in 1703. It was a location for walks, picnics, afternoon naps, and, with its large gallery, card playing. The plan was not very practical in spite of its

charm and beauty, and frequent rearrangements of the interior were made. At one point a theater was built; it can be distinguished in Le Nôtre's drawing in the wing near the basin shown on the upper left area of the plan.

G.W.

22.
Workshop of Jules Hardouin-Mansart (1646–1708)
France
Château de Clagny: Elevation of the Central Pavilion
Pen and black ink, gray wash; 39.8 × 55.5 cm.
Bibliography: Stockholm, 1942, no. 91; *Audran*, 1950, no. 209; Paris, 1951, no. 214; Paris, 1985, no. G5
Nationalmuseum, Stockholm, CC 312B

The fountains of Versailles were fed at first by pumping water up the hill from the Clagny pond north of the château. Louis XIV decided on the far side of the pond as the location for the house of his mistress Mme de Montespan. It seemed an ideal spot, convenient but slightly outside the royal domain. A first project was drawn up by Antoine Le Pautre, but according to the duc de Luynes, the plan was refused as suitable only for an opera singer—not at all correct for a woman from one of France's oldest and greatest families. Hardouin-Mansart saved the day in 1676 with a design for a far more splendid building, the central element of which is shown here. The Château de Clagny was known for its galleries and gardens. In 1687 Tessin reported that it was empty and in neglected condition— undoubtedly because of the fall from favor of the lady in question. Her son the duc de Maine inherited it, but the château has not survived.

G.W.

23.
J. Heulot the Younger
France, 1670s
Château de Marly: Plans and Elevations
Pen and brown ink, gray, green and rose wash; 42.5 × 23 cm.
Inscribed throughout and signed: *J. Heulot le Jeune*
Bibliography: Ragnar Josephson, "Le plan primitif de Marly," *Revue de l'histoire de Versailles*, 1928, pp. 27–44.; Paris, 1951, no. 231, Gerold Weber, "Der Garten von Marley (1679–1715)," *Wiener Jahrbuch für Kunstgeschichte* 28 (1975): 60–62; Betsy Rosasco, "The Sculptural Decoration of the Garden of Marly: 1679–1699," *Journal of Garden History* 4 (1984): 101, fig. 3; Paris, 1985, no. J1
Nationalmuseum, Stockholm, THC 25

When a controversy arose over whether the king should complete the chapel of Versailles in spite of the wretched state of the country, Mme de Maintenon remarked that the court might well move to Marly in any case. Marly was the preferred residence during the last years of the reign. There most etiquette was suspended and the king lived a relatively informal life with some invited friends. He and his immediate family lived in a large house located on the side of a hill, surrounded by a spectacular terraced landscape. The invited guests were lodged in twelve small two-story houses at the edge of the main axis, and they joined Louis for meals. Most buildings at Marly and some of the fountains were pulled down at the beginning of the nineteenth century.

22.

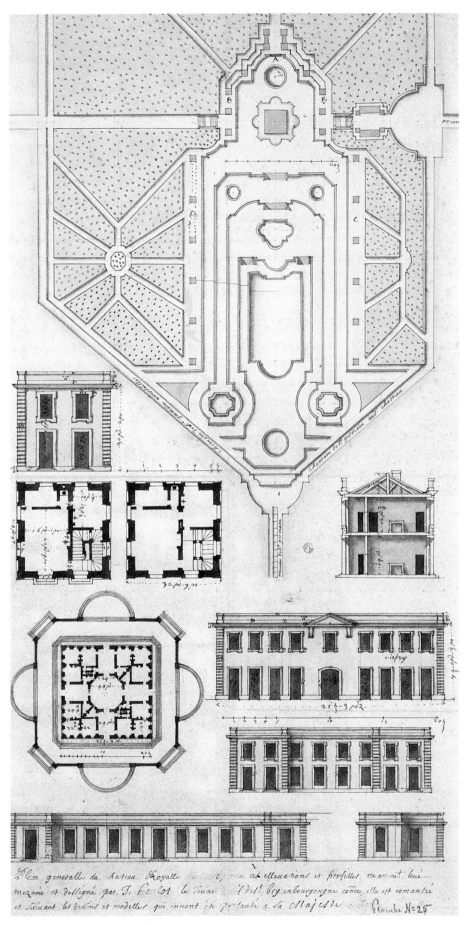

Plan generalle du hateau Royalle … e as elleuations et profilles ex are nt leué
mezure et dessigné par J. Ferlot le Veure J dct Vey enbourgongne cõme elle est comanté
et suiuant les dessins et modelles qui ennont été … à Sa Majesté Planche Nº 25

23.

24.

Heulot's drawing was at first taken as an accurate early plan (by Josephson), but Weber has shown that the treatment of the gardens differs significantly from the way they are rendered in a number of other early plans.
G.W.

24.
Unknown Draftsman
France, 1687–88
Château de Marly: Elevation of One of the Four Identical Façades
Pen and black ink, gray wash; 24.2 × 44.2 cm.
Bibliography: Stockholm, 1942, no. 61; Paris, 1985, no. J2
Nationalmuseum, Stockholm, CC 2206

The exteriors of the buildings at Marly were decorated with paintings, many after drawings by Charles Le Brun, probably in the 1670s. A complicated symbolic program governed this important painted decoration, but it is difficult to read in the drawing. The king's arms can be seen, and in the central pediment Apollo (the Sun and the emblem of Louis XIV) is shown in his chariot preceded by Aurora (Dawn) and followed by a figure who may be Day.
G.W.

25.
Unknown Draftsman
France, 1687–88
Château de Marly: Section
Pen and black ink, gray wash; 39.7 × 53.5 cm.
Bibliography: Paris, 1951, no. 212; Paris, 1985, no. J3
Nationalmuseum, Stockholm, THC 6690

At the center of this drawing of the Château de Marly is the salon where the king dined, shown as it appeared before 1700, when four of the doors were replaced by fireplaces. The two-story interior was lighted from above through windows on the second floor. Shown on either side of the central room are wall elevations of two of the four large vestibules that led from the central portals to the salon.

Tessin admired Marly and made a similar section sketch for his notes (see Paris, 1985, No. K2); he collected three interior elevations and three plans of the central pavilion and other plans of the gardens.
G.W.

26.
Unknown Artist
France, 1670s
Silver Bed
Red chalk, pen and black ink, watercolor, gold and silver paint; 42.9 × 55 cm.
Bibliography: Paris, 1951, no. 125; Thornton, 1978, p. 151, fig. 120; Stockholm, 1986, no. 61
Nationalmuseum, Stockholm, THC 1060

This drawing has been associated with a bed made for the French royal château of Saint-Germain-en-Laye, north of Versailles. Saint-Germain was Louis XIV's birthplace, and the château was lavishly refurbished by him soon after he began his personal rule in 1661. Only at Saint-Germain was there a place for the elaborate royal productions of operas during the 1670s and 1680s.

Thornton suggests that this might be a silver bed designed for Saint-Germain by Charles Le Brun in 1669.

Similar in type to some *lits de repos* at Trianon, the work shown is clearly a day bed rather than one for nighttime

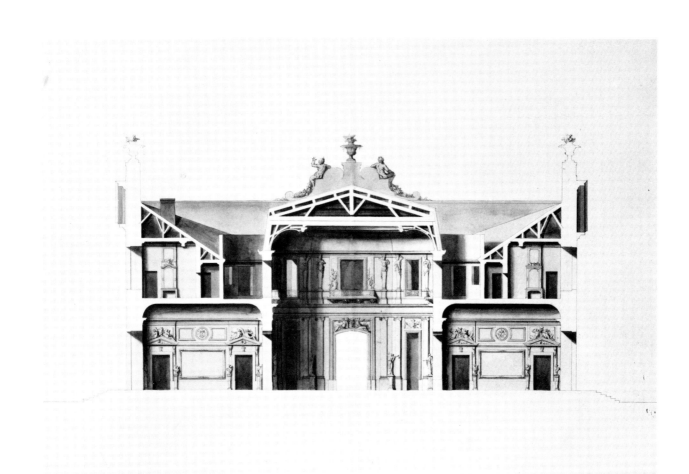

25.

26.

27.

sleeping. The connection with the royal piece remains conjectural, however. The image resembles the furniture to be seen in the popular ornamental engravings of the time such as those by Jean Le Pautre.
G.W.

27.
Charles Le Brun (1619–1690)
France
Candlestand
Red chalk, gray wash; 37.8 × 23.8 cm.
Verso: red chalk study of two figures
Bibliography: Paris, 1951, no. 123; *Le Brun*, 1963, no. 96; P. Bjurström, *French Drawings* . . ., Stockholm, 1976, no. 498; Thornton, 1978, p. 13, fig. 5; Paris, 1985, no. M10; Stockholm, 1986, no. 86
Nationalmuseum, Stockholm, CC 1751

Vaux-le-Vicomte was the country house built from 1656 to 1661 by the French finance minister Nicolas Fouquet. It was the first collaboration of the painter Charles Le Brun, the gardener André Le Nôtre, and the architect Louis Le Vau— three men who would play a fundamental role in the design of Versailles a few years later. Vaux may be considered a dress rehearsal for the enlightened patronage of French artists in the age of Louis XIV.

Jennifer Montagu and Per Bjurström (*Le Brun*, 1963) have demonstrated that this important drawing, by the hand of the artist, is a study for an object made for Vaux. Le Brun collaborated with Le Vau on the interiors, planning and executing a number of decorations.

In his capacity as chief designer of the Gobelins manufactory in the 1660s, Le Brun became one of the most influential designers of French furniture. This work of the late 1650s showing his earlier activity as a furniture designer explains Louis XIV's decision to place Le Brun in charge there.

The history of the candlestand depicted is unclear. It is not known whether the piece was executed or of what materials. If made in silver it could have passed into the royal collections later at Versailles, along with much else from Vaux, after the disgrace of Fouquet.
G.W.

28.
Claude Ballin (1615–1678) or Nicolas de Launay (died 1727)
France
Andiron for a Member of the Colbert Family
Pen and black ink, gray wash; 39.4 × 24.9 cm.
Inscribed: *Delaunay fecit*
Bibliography: Paris, 1951, no. 135; Hernmarck, 1953, p. 108, fig. 4; Paris, 1985, no. M1; Stockholm, 1986, no. 94
Nationalmuseum, Stockholm, THC 2109

In a letter written to Tessin on April 19, 1693, Daniel Cronström explained that he was sending to Stockholm a number of drawings by Louis XIV's great silversmith, Claude Ballin: "You will find at the bottom . . . the name de Launay who succeeded Baslin . . . but they are really by Baslin." (Weigert and Hernmarck, 1964, p.15) The attribution is complicated, since at least two groups of Ballin drawings were sent to Stockholm at different times, and a number of them represent objects in Ballin's style of the 1660s and 1670s.

De Launay was commissioned to do drawings after works by Ballin (specifically of the royal household's silver furniture, which was melted down in 1690), and it is possible that Cronström confused some of de Launay's copies with originals. It is tempting to attribute the more freely drawn sheets to the older master and the more carefully delineated ones, like this drawing, to de Launay.

The andiron may well have been executed in silver.
G.W.

29.
Attributed to Claude Ballin (1615–1678)
France
Andiron for a Member of the Colbert Family
Pen and black ink, black chalk, gray and brown wash; 33 × 22 cm.
Bibliography: Hernmarck, 1953, p. 109, fig. 5; Paris, 1985, no. M11; Stockholm, 1986, no. 95
Nationalmuseum, Stockholm, THC 1134

Carl Hernmarck suggests that this sheet is one of three sent by Cronström to Tessin in 1699. The bold, broad drawing style may indicate a working drawing by the master himself rather than a drawing made for the engraver. If it is for a work in silver, it would have been made before 1672, when strict measures were taken to prevent the making of such luxurious objects for private persons.
G.W.

30.
Claude Ballin (1615–1678)
France
Candlestand in the Form of a Moor
Pen and brown ink, black chalk, gray wash; 33.7 × 22.3 cm.
Inscribed: *Cinq pieds et demy de haut*
Bibliography: Hernmarck, 1953, p. 111, fig. 7; Hernmarck, 1977, II, fig. 516; Thornton, 1978, p. 26, fig. 25; Paris, 1985, no. M13; Stockholm, 1986, no. 88
Nationalmuseum, Stockholm, THC 1125

This splendid drawing, which relates closely to the previous sheet and may well be a study by Ballin himself, is similar to a composition engraved by Jean Le Pautre; however, in a number of details the ornament here differs from that in the print. It is possible that Le Pautre varied Ballin's design or that Ballin made more than one variation of the project.
G.W.

31.
After Claude Ballin (1615–1678)
France
Silver Table
Pen and black and brown ink; 40 × 56 cm.
Scale at lower right corner
Bibliography: Hernmarck, 1953, p. 116, fig. 10; Hermarck, 1977, II, fig. 518; Thornton, 1978, p. 234, fig. 220; Paris, 1985, no. M14; Stockholm, 1986, no. 85
Nationalmuseum, Stockholm, THC 1098

The crown and the lyres in the ornament as well as the arms of France shown at the center of the frieze below the tabletop

28.

29.

30.

31.

indicate that this is a drawing of an important piece of royal furniture. The unrefined drawing style would seem to indicate that the sheet is a representation of the piece rather than a design for it; possibly the drawing, which contains a scale, was done expressly for Sweden.
G.W.

32.
Claude Ballin (1615–1678) or Nicolas de Launay (died 1727)
France
Projects for Two Silver Tables or Consoles
Pen and black ink, gray wash; 42.5 × 35.3 cm.
Bibliography: Paris, 1951, no, 114; *Le Brun*, 1963, p. 281; A. and J. Marie, 1972, II, p. 486; Thornton, 1978, p. 15, fig. 10; Paris, 1985, no. M2; Stockholm, 1986, no. 82
Nationalmuseum, Stockholm, CC 2389

The left half of the lower table design has been identified by Peter Thornton as having been shown in a Sébastien Le Clerc (1637–1714) engraving of the Hall of Mirrors. In 1687 Tessin counted 190 pieces of solid-silver furniture in the Grand Apartment of Versailles, many in the Hall of Mirrors. This furniture was among the wonders of the palace, and its melting in January 1690, forced by financial considerations, was considered an artistic tragedy.

It is nonetheless difficult to tell what this drawing represents. It may indicate designs for four different consoles for the Hall of Mirrors, or it may relate to an earlier commission showing four possibilities. Charles Le Brun, as the first painter and head of the Gobelins manufactory in Paris, would certainly have wished to be involved in designing the furniture for the Hall of Mirrors, a gallery for which he had executed an immense ceiling painting, but the style of the drawing itself is not his and remains most comfortably placed in the group attributed to Ballin and/or de Launay (see No. 28).
G.W.

33.
Claude Ballin (1615–1678) or Nicolas de Launay (died 1727)
France
Alternative Projects for a Candlestand
Pen and black ink, gray wash; 49.3 × 31.7 cm.
Bibliography: *Le Brun*, 1963, no. 120, fig. 8; Thornton, 1978, p. 14, fig. 8; Paris, 1985, no. M3; Stockholm, 1986, no. 87
Nationalmuseum, Stockholm, CC 2419

An object of this type, presumably by Ballin, is shown in a Gobelins tapestry after Le Brun representing an interior of the Louvre from the *Histoire du roi* series. It appears to be of silver and about five feet tall. Such stands were also used in the king's Audience Room at Versailles.

The drawing is similar in draftsmanship to Nos. 28 and 32. It shows either alternatives for the patron's choice or two slightly different objects.

A classic of the Gobelins style during Le Brun's direction of the manufactory, this candlestand is considered to be one of the finest of the designs for Louis XIV's silver furniture.
G.W.

32.

33.

34.
Nicolas de Launay? (died 1727)
France
Silver Chandelier
Pen and brown ink, gray wash; 47.5 × 33 cm.
Bibliography: Paris, 1951, no. 116; Hernmarck, 1953, p. 118, fig. 12;
 Thornton, 1978, p. 273, fig. 263; Paris, 1985, no. M5; Stockholm,
 1986, no. 92
Nationalmuseum, Stockholm, CC 1549

The royal inventories of France of February 1681 mention a chandelier with six branches that has been identified with the object shown on this sheet although only two branches appear here and the figure of Fame at the top is not mentioned in the inventory. In the issue of the *Mercure gallant* of 1682, in which the Grand Apartment of Louis XIV is described in detail, mention is made of a silver chandelier, with a figure of Fame, hanging in the Salon of Mercury, where the state bed was set up. These documents suggest that the drawing is that extreme rarity—a record of one of the famous solid-silver furnishings of Versailles, drawn by de Launay for the engraver before the work was melted down. This appears to be a hand similar to that of Nos. 28, 32, 33, and 35.
G.W.

35.
Nicolas de Launay? (died 1727)
France
Console
Pen and brown ink, gray wash; 33 × 46 cm.
Bibliography: Paris, 1951, no. 113; Hernmarck, 1953, p. 117, fig. 11;
 Hernmarck, 1977, II, fig. 519; Paris, 1985, no. M6; Stockholm,
 1986, no. 84
Nationalmuseum, Stockholm, CC 3187

Close in quality and style to the previous drawing and on the same kind of paper, this sheet shows alternative designs for consoles of the type fabricated in silver for Versailles. A diagram of the lower support seen from above appears sketchily rendered below the highly finished image of the console. The fact that this manner of showing details not otherwise visible was frequently used by engravers strengthens the argument that this sheet and No. 34 were drawings of the Versailles silver furniture made by de Launay for the engraver (see No. 28). Similar consoles were used in a number of rooms of the Grand Apartment of the King, and the style here is also close to that of the pieces shown in Le Clerc's engraving of the Hall of Mirrors.
G.W.

36.
Unknown Draftsman
France, 1702
Diagram of the Table Setting at Marly
Pen and black ink; 15 × 22.5 cm.
Inscribed throughout and dated
Bibliography: Paris, 1985, no. N4; Stockholm, 1986, no. 102a
Nationalmuseum, Stockholm, THC 2099

At Marly the usual number of people at each of the two tables used for meals was eighteen or nineteen. The tables were oval, and serving dishes of food were arranged in carefully

34.

35.

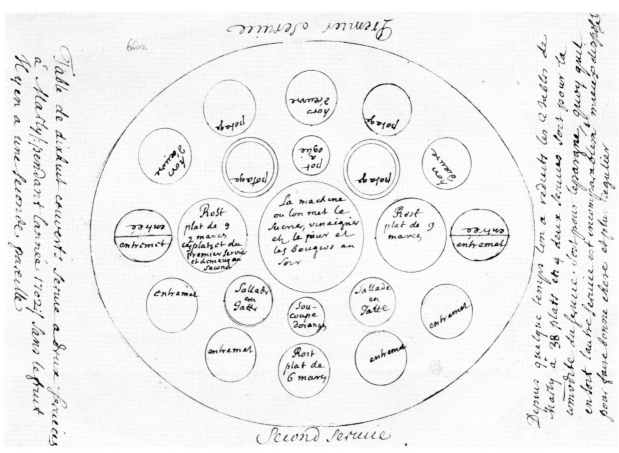

Premier service

Second service

662

La machine ou l'on met le beure, vinaigre et le pain et les bougies au soir

Rost plat de 9 marcs deplats et du premier service et donne au second

Rost plat de 9 marcs

Rost plat de 6 marcs

Sallade en Jatte

Sallade en Jatte

Soucoupe d'orange

entremet · entremet · entremet · entremet · entremet · entremet

potage · potage · potage · potage

pot a oille · roy Seurm · roy Seurm · roy Seurm

Depuis quelque temps l'on a reduit les 2 tables de Marly a 38 plats et 4 deux services sont pour la comodité du service; sont pour epargne, quoy qu'il en soit l'autre service est incomparablement mieux ordonné pour faire bonne chere et plus regulier

Table de dixhuit couverts servie a deux services a Marty; pendant l'année 1702; sans le fruit Il y en a une seconde, pareille

36.

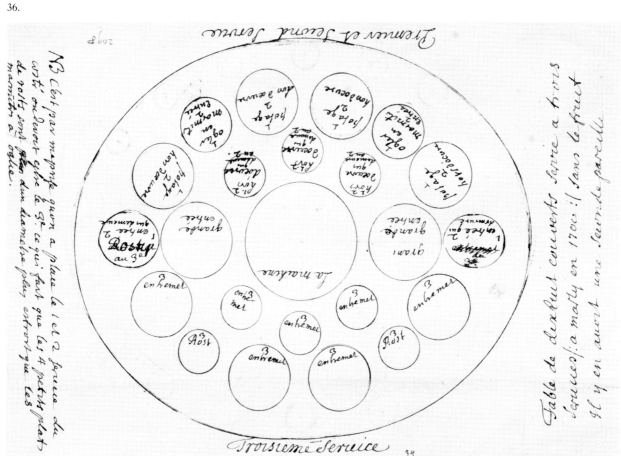

Premier et Second service

Troisieme Service

698

34

La machine

grande entrée · grande entrée · grand entrée

Rost · Rost · entremet · entremet · entremet · entremet · entremet · entremet · entremet · entremet

NB C'est par ma propre qu'on a placé le 1 et 2 service du 3e service; a Marty en 1700; sans le fruit Il y en avait une seconde pareille

NB C'est par ma propre qu'on a placé le 1 et 2 service art. on devoit estre le 9e ce qui fait que les 4 petits plats de potz sont bien dun diametre plus etroit que les 8 marmites à oille.

Table de dixhuit couverts servie a trois services; a Marty en 1700; sans le fruit Il y en avait une seconde pareille

37.

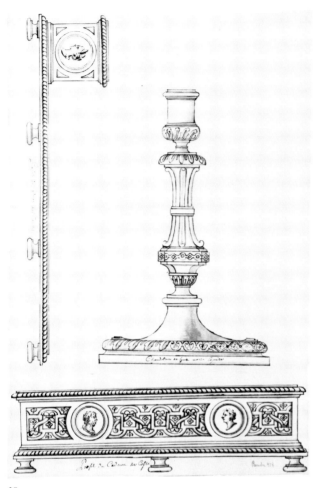

38.

calculated patterns to produce a pyramidal effect. Presumably, one talked with one's neighbor and not across the table. These artful arrangements are recorded in this and a few other diagrams obtained by the Swedish court in 1702.

The arrangement of the table at Marly was not at all like that at Versailles, where Louis ate by himself or with the king and queen of England (James II and Mary of Modena, who were in exile). There large plates and dishes were arranged somewhat haphazardly on a rectangular table, though much of the same table service was used.

The Marly table resembled those depicted in the engravings of Versailles fêtes of the 1660s and 1670s. This similarity may be explained by the fact that a visit to Marly was an escape from the usual court ritual and very much of a social event.

This drawing and No. 37 were probably acquired as a result of Tessin's request to Cronström for information about Louis XIV's table. At first the royal household refused permission for Cronström's draftsmen to draw the royal silver, but in 1702 it was eventually granted. As a result the Stockholm collection contains the most complete surviving information on the Sun King's table.
G.W.

37.
Unknown Draftsman
France, 1700
The Table at Marly
Pen and black ink, black chalk; 15 × 22.2 cm
Inscribed throughout and dated
Bibliography: Paris 1985, no. N5; Stockholm, 1986, no. 102b
Nationalmuseum, Stockholm, THC 2098

This diagram is dated 1700. It contains a curious inscription, which translates, "N.B. It is by error that they put the first and second services where the third ought to be." This statement seems to mean that the draftsmen, rather than the royal household, were at fault. It appears that two or three courses were on the table at once, and were probably uncovered at the appropriate times. A separate setting for the fruit and the sweets was apparently used.
G.W.

38.
Nicolas-Amboise Cousinet
France, 1702
Cadenas and Candlestick
Pen and black ink, gray wash; 38.3 × 24.5
Inscribed: *Profil du Cadenas de Costé/Chandelier de huit ma . . . la paire / Profil de Cadenas de Travers*
Bibliography: Hernmarck, 1977, II, fig. 396; Paris, 1985, no. N8; Stockholm, 1986, no. 104
Nationalmuseum, Stockholm, THC 818

In May 1702, Cronström received permission to have an artist draw the plate used on the French king's table. He engaged Cousinet, a little-known member of a famous family of silversmiths, to do the drawings for him.

A *cadenas* (a box attached to a tray) held the king's knife, spoon, and, possibly, a fork. This vessel was a modest survival of the tradition of the elaborate *nef*s (ships) of silver and gold used by late medieval kings. The cadenas was set at the right of the king's place at the table.

It is impossible to attribute the pieces drawn by Cousinet to one silversmith or another, though it is certain that a number were made from the designs of Jean I Berain, the designer of silver and the *menus plaisirs* of the king's chamber. The king's table undoubtedly included some pieces made before Berain's time and others acquired from diverse sources. Much of what Cousinet drew was melted down in 1707 during the War of Spanish Succession (1701–14). G.W.

39.

39.
Nicolas-Amboise Cousinet
France, 1702
Silver-Gilt and Silver Pieces from Louis XIV's Petit Couvert
Pen and black ink, black chalk, gray wash; 51 × 38.5 cm.
Verso: sauceboat, salt and pepper containers, tray
Inscribed: *Au Roy / pour le petit couvert du Roy.* and throughout
Bibliography: Weigert, 1931, pl. 1; A. and J. Marie, 1972, II, pp. 329, 330; Hernmarck, 1977, II, fig. 411; Paris, 1985, no. N10; Stockholm, 1986, no. 106
Nationalmuseum, Stockholm, THC 774, 775

The *Petit Couvert* of Louis XIV refers to the evening meal that the king ate alone or with the king of England. The *Grand Couvert* was the midday meal taken with the queen or other members of the family. After 1683 the *Petit Couvert* took place in the king's first antechamber at Versailles. A member of the king's family was present, standing, to hand the king his napkin while the court stood around the room to watch him eat. It was a tradition that courtiers bowed as the *viandes du roi* (the king's meat) passed by.

The round objects shown in the diagrams of the royal table were more often than not trays that contained a number of vessels for different kinds of food. Several medium-sized trays of this sort would have been on the table, while a larger one with candelabra and dishes would have served as a centerpiece. The two-handled vessel in the drawing is a covered bowl for oil.

The inscription *Au Roy* on this sheet verifies that these pieces were indeed Louis XIV's. Other table services, such as that of the duc d'Aumont, were recorded by Cousinet in this same series of drawings, but the owners are always indicated. Three different hands have made notes on this sheet and on many of the others from the Cousinet group. The remarks range widely in subject and suggest that those who wrote were not sure what was needed in Stockholm. G.W.

40.
Nicolas-Amboise Cousinet
France, 1702
Silver Pieces for the Table and Sideboard
Pen and black ink, gray wash; 37.4 × 50 cm.
Verso: teapot and diagram of tray with cups
Inscribed: *Duc Daumont; Enguive pour mettre sur le buffet . . . / Plan de la poiviere a trois au Roy / Profil de la poiviere . . .*
Bibliography: Hernmarck, 1977, II, figs. 306, 443, 667; Paris, 1985, no. N11; Stockholm, 1986, no. 107
Nationalmuseum, Stockholm, THC 2106, 2107, 2108

Louis XIV's three-part saltcellar is the most important item

40. recto

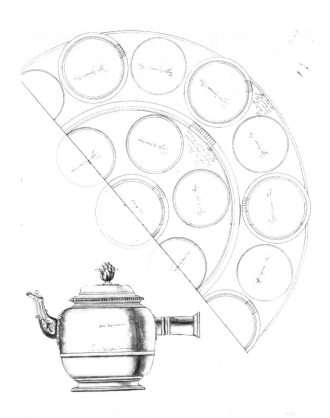

40. verso

on this sheet, along with a splendid pitcher in Berain's style from the sideboard of the duc d'Aumont. The duc d'Aumont's teapot and a diagram for a tray holding numerous circular objects are drawn on the verso.
G.W.

41.
Nicolas-Amboise Cousinet
France, 1702
Coffeepot, Bouillon Pot, Sugar Caster, and Flatware
Pen and black ink, watercolor; 50 × 38.5 cm.
Verso: teapot, candlestick, and wine cooler
Inscribed: The note *au Roy* appears on the pieces, identified as a *Pot à bouillon* and *sucrier*; other inscriptions identify the uses of the various objects
Bibliography: Weigert, 1931, pl. 5; Hernmarck, 1977, II, figs. 340, 430; Paris, 1985, no. N12; Stockholm, 1986, no. 108
Nationalmuseum, Stockholm, THC 833–36

This sheet shows a coffeepot, a pot for bouillon, a sugar caster, and a fine teapot and other items from the table of the duchesse de Lude on the verso. The quality of all of these designs is outstanding, though the greatest interest of this drawing is its use of color, which indicates that the objects were enameled. The royal inventories published by Jules Guiffrey in Paris (1885) often mention the enameled silver of the king, but no pieces have survived and there are few other indications of its appearance.
G.W.

41. recto

42.
Nicolas-Amboise Cousinet
France, 1702
Silver Fruit Basket and a Plate
Pen and black ink, watercolor; 55 × 38.5 cm.
Verso: plan of the king's table at Marly and a plate
Inscribed throughout
Bibliography: Weigert, 1931, pl. 5; A. and J. Marie, 1972, II, p. 329; Paris, 1985, no. N13; Stockholm, 1986, no. 109
Nationalmuseum, Stockholm, THC 831, 832

This sheet shows a spectacular silver fruit basket that could also be used for candied fruit. A note mentions that the basket could be used for fish, as well. The top view and profile of a silver plate are also shown on the front of the sheet, and another plate is depicted on the verso. These were obviously major pieces of silver that decorated Louis XIV's table. Sometimes porcelain dessert cups replaced the silver ones shown here.
G.W.

41. verso

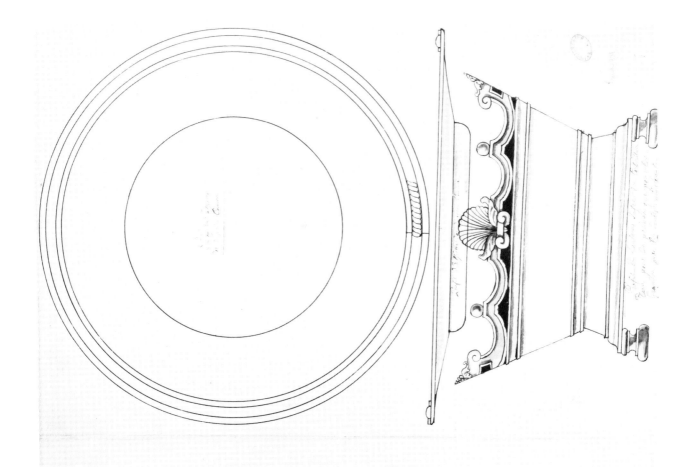

Nota que ce profil de corbeille et de tasses
n'ent point dans les mesures, et n'est fait
que pour donner l'intelligence de la maniere
d'arranger le fruit, et de poser les tasses
et gobelets marqués dans le plan

Profil de la Corbeille Garnye
de fruit crud

Profil de la Corbeille Garnye
de tasses et gobelets pour les six
quatres. Il fé pose des Confitures
sèche. Il fé mes Deux tasses
de gueridons pour les milieu auffi
garny de Confitures sèche

43.
Nicolas-Amboise Cousinet
France, 1702
Two-tiered Silver Tray for Candy
Pen and black ink, gray wash; 38.3 × 49.8 cm.
Inscribed: *Profile du Plat du premier rang a Confissure . . ., Pour le grand*
    Couvert à Versailles et à Marly
Bibliography: Weigert, 1931, pl. 1; Paris, 1985, no. N14; Stockholm,
    1986, no. 110
Nationalmuseum, Stockholm, THC 798

The inscription identifies this piece as having been used for
the *Grand Couvert* at both Versailles and Marly.
G.W.

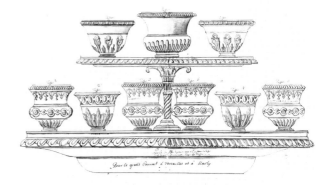

43.

44.
Jean I Berain (1640–1711)
France
Silver Pitcher
Pen and black ink, gray wash; 40.2 × 26.7 cm.
Inscribed: *L'aunay*
Bibliography: Paris, 1985, no. O1; Stockholm, 1986, no. 111; de La
    Gorce, 1986, p. 52
Nationalmuseum, Stockholm, THC 790

Jérôme de La Gorce has recently identified this sheet as the
work of Jean Berain (executed by him in part) despite the
inscription naming de Launay. This work might have been
one of those mentioned in the Cronström-Tessin correspondence as being sent to Sweden in 1694, but Berain drawings
were sent to Stockholm on a number of occasions. De La
Gorce suggests a date of 1702.
G.W.

45.
Jean I Berain (1640–1711)
France
Candelabrum
Pen and black ink, gray wash; 39.5 × 35.2 cm.
Bibliography: Paris, 1985, no. O2
Nationalmuseum, Stockholm, THC 812

This curious object is a highly original design. The top center
part resembles an inkwell, but it is difficult to imagine this
round object on a desk. There is no clue to identify the
patron. The ornament has the originality and vigor of Berain's
style, and the drawing technique is consistent with his work.
G.W.

45.

46.
Unknown Artist "A"
France, c. 1700
Silver Tray with Three Goblets
Pen and black ink, black chalk, gray wash; 20. 5 × 25.2 cm.
Inscribed: *4*
Bibliography: Paris, 1985, no. O3; Stockholm, 1986, no. 112
Nationalmuseum, Stockholm, THC 849

Groups of anonymous drawings of silver by the same hand
may be distinguished in the Nationalmuseum collection.
The drawings in the series by the artist designated "A" are
numbered and are on the same kind of French paper. It is
impossible to identify the draftsman or the silver designer

46

Launay.

Planho 790.

44.

since it is quite possible that Cronström commissioned drawings of works by a number of silversmiths.
G.W.

47.
Unknown Artist "A"
France, c. 1700
Warming Stand and Lamp
Pen and black ink, black chalk, gray wash; 19 × 26 cm.
Inscribed: *2*
Bibliography: Paris, 1985, no. O4
Nationalmuseum, Stockholm, THC 840

48.
Unknown Artist "A"
France, c. 1700
Silver Wine Cooler
Pen and black ink, black chalk; 29.7 × 25 cm.
Inscribed: *2*
Bibliography: Paris, 1985, no. O5; Stockholm, 1986, no. 113
Nationalmuseum, Stockholm, THC 776

This is a classic example of French silver design of about 1700. A pair of coolers of similar design was made in France for the Swedish Piper family in 1702 (see Stockholm, 1986, No. 37). Works that closely resemble this piece were being made by Huguenot silversmiths in London at the time.
G.W.

49.
Unknown Artist "B"
France, c. 1700
Warming Stand and Lamp
Pen and black ink, gray wash; 24.5 × 42 cm.
Inscribed: *2 Reschauds*
Bibliography: Paris, 1985, no. 07
Nationalmuseum, Stockholm, THC 807

This is one of another group of works identifiable by inscriptions and numbers. Though by a different hand, it is drawn on the same kind of paper as group "A."
G.W.

50–56.
Nicolas de Launay (died 1727)
France
The Oxenstierna Silver Dressing-Table Set
Pen and black and brown ink, gray and brown wash, black chalk;
    each 22.5 × 13.7 cm.
Inscribed throughout
Bibliography: R.-A. Weigert, *Jean I Berain*, Paris, 1937, figs. 35, 36;
    Weigert and Hernmarck, 1964, pp. 104, 126–27; Hernmarck, 1977,
    II, figs. 704–7; Paris, 1985, nos. Q1–7; Stockholm, 1986, nos.
    114–20
Nationalmuseum, Stockholm, THC 843, 842, 1099, 803, 851, 841,
    856

On May 21, 1696, Daniel Cronström wrote to Tessin that Nicolas de Launay was the greatest of the French silversmiths, even better than Berain for silver designs. Louis XIV seems to have agreed: when he gradually set about replacing the table silver, which had been melted down in

47.

48.

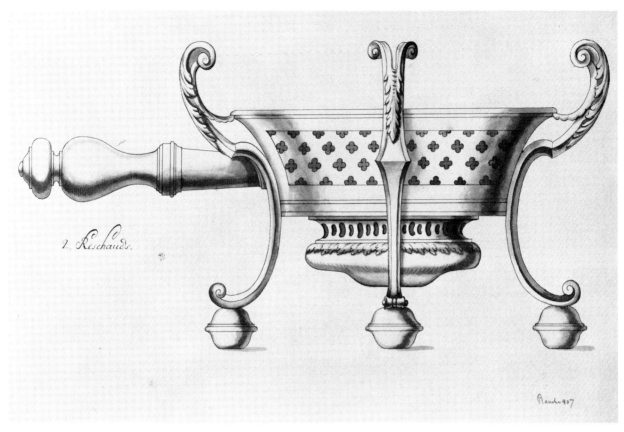

2. Réchauds.

Rendu 407

49.

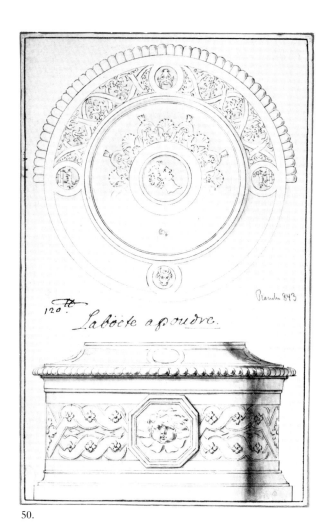

50.

51.

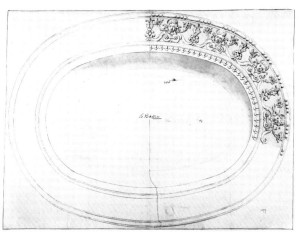

52.

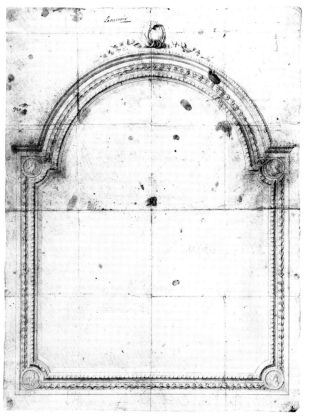

53.

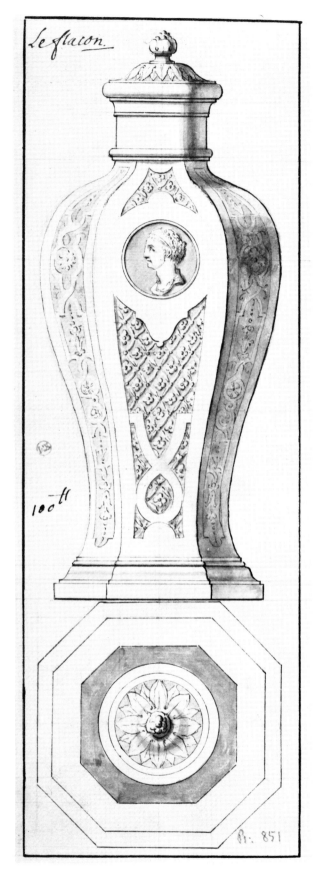

Le flacon.

100 H

B: 851

54.

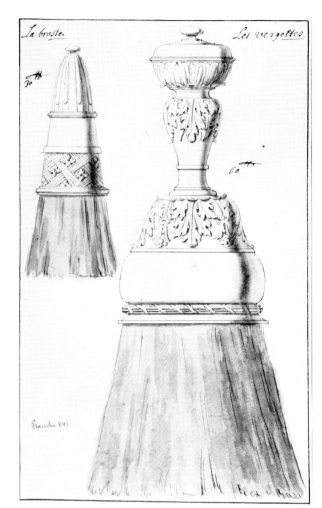

La brosse. *Les vergettes.*

30

60

Planche 841

55.

L'aiguière.

100

Planche 876

56.

1707, he often turned to de Launay, who was paid for deliveries between 1709 and 1715.

Among the many silver drawings in Stockholm are seven that, only recently recognized, must rank among the silversmith's greatest works. None of his silver seems to have survived. The drawings were designs for the dressing table of Countess Oxenstierna, née Steinbock, one of the richest women in Sweden.

In 1695 the countess or her husband approached Tessin to find out whether he could obtain designs by a great French silversmith that could be executed in Stockholm. In January 1696 Cronström announced from Paris the good news that de Launay himself had agreed to supply the drawings. In the end, it proved difficult to extract the designs, and a certain amount of deception became necessary. In May 1696 Cronström wrote: "Launay is persuaded that this is for the Queen [the dowager queen of Sweden, Hedvig Eleanora]." There were other problems: silversmiths disliked making designs that they would not execute, and goat and ox heads (motifs referring to the lady's name) were not beautiful motifs to incorporate in the ornament of silver objects to be used in the bedroom. Finally the drawings were sent to Stockholm, but it is not known whether the silver was ever made.

The set includes the following items: a silver powder box (50); a small chest (for jewelry?) with a pincushion on the top (51); a deep oval silver bowl for washing (52); a mirror (53); a perfume bottle (54); two brushes to remove the powder from clothes after the makeup was applied (55); and a ewer (56).

The creation of such important silver for the bedroom of a countess had less to do with the lady's vanity than with court ceremony. The nobility appeared in the presence of the monarch in court dress and jewelry on many occasions; thus, dressing was a part of the homage due to the sovereign, and, therefore, an activity worthy of such elaborate trappings.
G.W.

57.

57.
Jean I Berain (1640–1711)
France
Pair of Consoles Surmounted by Ornamental Vases
Pen and brown ink, brown wash; 46.8 × 29 cm.
Bibliography: A. and J. Marie, 1976, p. 205, fig. 87; Paris, 1985, no. P1; Stockholm, 1986, no. 97
Nationalmuseum, Stockholm, THC 8611

This design is a particularly fine example of both Berain's draftsmanship and his genius as an ornamentalist. Alfred Marie believes that he has identified the works made from it in an old photograph of the Oval Salon of the Versailles Zoo. Although his identification would seem to be correct, it should be remembered that consoles were applied to the wall against mirrors for decorative effect in many rooms at Versailles: the Council Chamber, the Cabinet of Herms, and the Billiard Room.
G.W.

58.

59.

58.
Jean I Berain (1640–1711)
France
Console
Pen and brown ink, brown wash; 28.3 × 27.2 cm.
Bibliography: Paris, 1951, no. 132; Paris, 1985, no. P2; Stockholm, 1986, no. 98
Nationalmuseum, Stockholm, THC 1073

This sheet is another in the splendid series of drawings that Berain dispatched to Tessin. Tessin, who had met Berain in Paris, spoke of his *beau genie*. All three console designs appear in an etching after Berain by Marguerin Daigremont.
G.W.

59.
Unknown Artist
France or Sweden, c. 1700
Console
Pen and black ink, gray wash; 26.5 × 26.5 cm.
Bibliography: Paris, 1985, no. P3
Nationalmuseum, Stockholm, THC 1131

The English paper used here suggests that this work was not made in France. Its presence in Stockholm would seem to indicate that the draftsman was a Swedish follower of Berain, though the possibility that he was a French or other foreign artist working in Stockholm cannot be excluded.
G.W.

60.
Jean I Berain (1640–1711)
France
Versailles: Clock for the Small Gallery
Pen and black ink, brown, gray and pink wash; 83.5 × 48.7 cm.
Inscribed on plans; scale
Bibliography: de La Gorce, 1986, pp. 48–49
Nationalmuseum, Stockholm, THC 1135

Possibly the most important piece of furniture designed by Berain, this clock was made for the Small Gallery, a large room adjoining the Stairway of the Ambassadors on the second floor of the château at Versailles. The room was best known for a famous ceiling executed by Pierre Mignard (1612–95) and for its sumptuous wall decorations made at the Gobelins manufactory. The wall decorations, when exhibited in Paris, caused a sensation for their richness and originality, but they subsequently disappeared and were never installed in the château. Both the stairway and the Small Gallery were torn down during the reign of Louis XV. It is not certain that the clock actually was a royal commission, and as Jérôme de La Gorce has noted, the piece remained in the artist's hands until his death. Berain had asked six thousand livres for it—an enormous sum that was apparently more than could be accepted. At his death in 1711 it was valued at two thousand livres. The clock eventually belonged to the duc d'Aumont and his descendants.

Not only was this drawing made for presentation to a patron, but as de La Gorce has discovered, a model of it was made by Pierre Le Nècre and Sébastien Slodtz. The symbolic program is restricted here to a few details such as the lyre of Apollo and a figure of Father Time seated on a globe.

60.

a fonds jaune pareil
a celuy des formes /

Le roy desiré cette bordure
trois dessings differents pour faire
deux tapis de chasun dessing /

61.

Other elements, such as the enameled blue and gold celestial globe on the top, may also have had a symbolic meaning, but they were actually part of the mechanism of the clock as well. Great care was taken to assure the highest possible quality of the work, particularly of the wood inlay and the metalwork. The clock is either lost or destroyed.
G.W.

61.
Attributed to Jean I Berain (1640–1711)
France
Design for a Savonnerie Carpet
Pen and brown ink, black chalk, watercolor; 19 × 35.7 cm.
Inscribed: *a fonds jaune pareil / a celui des formes / Le roi desiré cette bordure / trois dessings differents pour faire / deux tapis de chacun dessing.*
Bibliography: Madeleine Jarry, "Designs and Models for Savonnerie Carpets in the Eighteenth Century," *Burlington Magazine* 110 (1968): 258, fig. 29; Paris, 1951, no. 142; Stockholm, 1986, no. 18
Nationalmuseum, Stockholm, THC 1588

The inscription on the drawing bears witness to Louis XIV's wish to be involved in every aspect of the building and decoration of his residences. The artist offered two possibilities for the border of the carpet, and the king indicated his choice of the one at the right.

The design corresponds to a carpet listed in the royal inventory as being in the Billiard Room of the Grand Trianon and is similar to carpets by Charles Le Brun.
E.E.D.

62.
Workshop of Jean I Berain (1640–1711)
France
Design for a Tapestry Border
Black chalk, pen and gray / black ink, watercolor; 78 × 44.1 cm.
Bibliography: J. Böttiger, *Svenska statens samling af Väfda tapeter*, Stockholm, 1895, II, pp. 81–88; A. Setterwall, *Berains brodyrteckninger . . .*, Malmö, 1948, pp. 84–97, figs. 85, 87; Weigert and Hernmarck, 1964, pp. 84, 104, 163, 169, 172; Stockholm, 1986, no. 138
Nationalmuseum, Stockholm, THC 1179

The idea of making a series of tapestries depicting the victories of King Charles XI (1655–97) of Sweden in the war with Denmark (1675– 79) was put forward by Nicodemus Tessin the Younger in July 1695. The hangings were to be modeled on the recently completed series of paintings at Drottningholm Palace by Johan Philip Lemke (1631–1711). These in turn reproduce closely the drawings made by the quartermaster general Erik Dahlbergh, the king's close collaborator during the campaigns.

It was decided to have the tapestries made in France, where the best workmen were to be found. The commission would also provide an opportunity to make the Swedish king's military achievements better known there. The work dragged on, and only four of the planned series of ten were ever finished; the first two were delivered in 1699 and 1703, and the last two about 1705. The progress of the work can be followed in great detail in the correspondence between Tessin and Cronström.

The designs for the borders were commissioned from Jean Berain, and several alternatives were discussed during 1696 and 1697. Early in May 1697 Cronström sent Tessin a set of drawings, including Berain's autograph sketches in pen and

ink as well as larger, colored drawings that Cronström had also commissioned. In the end, a solution with flanking columns and large figures seated in front of the bases was adopted. The present drawing, where the ornament is arranged on the surface and the figures are much smaller, was suggested as an alternative, designed not to interfere with the main composition. Although it was not used, the drawing is a good example of the light and elegant designs that Berain provided Tessin.

B.M.

63.
Jean I Berain (1640–1711)
France
Water Spirit
Line engraving, watercolor; height 20.5 cm., sihouetted
Nationalmuseum, Stockholm, THC 3376

The rich collection of costume drawings by Jean Berain and his workshop provides a good idea of his working method. When a new costume was created, he often used an engraved outline such as on this sheet. Although barely visible, a figure in a dance position is discernible through the color. Jean Berain seems to have worked over original prints and on counterproofs, which together then form pairs.

The character might possibly have been a follower of the river Sanger in Jean-Baptiste Lully's opera *Atys*, performed for the king at Saint-Germain-en-Laye on January 10, 1676.

P.B.

64.
Jean I Berain (1640–1711)
France
Two Designs for Architects' Costumes
Sanguine, pen and black ink, gray wash; 22.7 × 15.2 cm., silhouetted
Bibliography: R.-A. Weigert, *Jean I Berain*, Paris, 1937, II, no. 206; *Sixteenth & Seventeenth Century Theatre Design in Paris*, London, Arts Council, 1956, no. 60; *Théâtre et fêtes à Paris XVIe et XVII siècles, Dessins du Musée National de Stockholm*, Paris, Musée Carnavalet, 1956, no. 85
Nationalmuseum, Stockholm, 17a:81/1874 and 82b:80/1874

These drawings are from a group, some of which have been engraved, that Weigert describes as "costumes for masquerades or ballets, symbolizing the professions allied to the arts and crafts." Architecture was included in the ballet *Le Triomphe des Arts*, of 1700, composed by Michel de la Barre. These drawings, probably by Berain himself, are variations on a theme. The right-hand figure was engraved by Jacques Le Pautre.

P.B.

63.

64.

65.

66.

65.
Workshop of Jean I Berain (1640–1711)
France
Equerry to the Dauphin
Pen and black ink, watercolor; 40 × 33.2 cm.
Inscribed on separate piece of paper, pasted on: *Couleur de Chair et argent / Escuyer de Monseigneur.*
Bibliography: London, 1956, no. 53; Paris, 1956, no. 78
Nationalmuseum, Stockholm, THC 5442

The drawing forms part of a group depicting the costumes of the Dauphin and his quadrille, the troop of riders that performed in the horse ballet. These drawings have been identified with those for the *Carrousel des galants maures* (Carrousel of the Moorish Gallants) of 1685, but they do not agree with the published descriptions of the carrousel by Donneau de Vizé. It is not known if the costumes for this carrousel were in fact made from these drawings, but they are probably of the same date.

The drawings were copies made by some artist in Berain's studio from the master's sketches. We can follow the negotiations in Daniel Cronström's letters to Nicodemus Tessin the Younger. He wrote on December 18, 1683: "I reminded him [Berain] of his Carousel. He promised me to have copies made for you. . . . He showed them to me. I asked him how much it would cost to have copies made. He told me at the least 8 *tt* per piece because it was necessary to mark all the colors. I don't know if you will not find this a little expensive; as for myself, I think it is. I will be guided by whatever you say. There are many more men than women. He said that most of the women had lost his drawings." Tessin answered on January 3, 1684: "Providing that the drawings of Monseigneur's Carousel are good copies with their colors, I will pay the 8 *tt* mentioned for each piece. I prefer the drawings of

women to those of men, however, not to reject the latter particularly when there are drawings with a man and a woman together" (Weigert and Hernmarck, 1964, pp. 37, 43).
P.B.

66.
Workshop of Jean I Berain (1640–1711)
France
Equerry to the Dauphin
Line engraving, watercolor; 39.4 × 28 cm.
Nationalmuseum, Stockholm, THC 4903

67.
Workshop of Jean I Berain (1640–1711)
France
State Coach for Charles XI: Side View
Pen and black ink, watercolor; 44.7 × 58.7 cm.
Inscribed on verso: *II*
Bibliography: For early references see Paris, 1985, no. R2; Tydén-Jordan, 1985; Stockholm, 1986, no. 73; de La Gorce, 1986, pp. 54, 55
Nationalmuseum, Stockholm, THC 943

After a fire destroyed the royal stables in Stockholm in February 1696, burning the coronation coaches of Charles XI, it was decided to commission a replacement in Paris, where the art of coach making had evolved rapidly in the previous decade. Louis XIV's own coach maker—probably François II Maillard, according to Rudolf Wackernagel (*Der französische Krönungswagen . . .*, Berlin, 1966, p. 66)—was engaged. Astrid Tydén-Jordan has identified a drawing, which she believes was worked up by François II Francart, that shows the latest

67.

type of coach being built at the time in Parisian workshops; that drawing was apparently transformed and refined aesthetically by Jean Berain, who was engaged to work out the complete details of the form of the coach and to provide an elaborate symbolic ornamental program that would suggest the autocratic power and the military achievements of Charles XI. Berain worked on the project throughout the summer of 1696, and in August a number of drawings, including this one, were sent to Stockholm.

The decision was made to send the coach to Stockholm before the painted and embroidered decorations conceived by Berain were executed, so the coach itself with its windows, wheels, and a remarkable floor probably by André-Charles Boulle, was made in Paris and sent to Sweden from Rouen in November 1696. The death of Charles XI in 1697 delayed the completion of this work and necessitated some changes in Berain's symbolic program, which had to be redesigned to celebrate the marriage of the young Charles XII (ruled 1697–1718), rather than the achievements of his father. The coach was completed in 1699.

Though substantially altered for a Swedish coronation of 1751, the coach remains in the Royal Palace and is on view at the Royal Livery.

The decoration was executed, in its broad lines, after Berain's designs, under the supervision of Nicodemus Tessin the Younger in Stockholm. The work was carried out by French artists working for the Swedish royal household. The design called for a combination of relief sculpture, cast metal, painting, and embroidery.
A. T.-J. and G.W.

68.

68.
Workshop of Jean I Berain (1640–1711)
France
State Coach for Charles XI: Front
Pen and black ink, watercolor; 41.2 × 28.4 cm.
Bibliography: See cat. no. 67
Nationalmuseum, Stockholm, THC 929

69.
Workshop of Jean I Berain (1640–1711)
France
State Coach for Charles XI: Rear View
Pen and black ink, black and red chalk, watercolor; 42.2 × 28.5 cm.
Bibliography: For early references see Paris, 1985, no. R4; Stockholm, 1986, no. 75; de La Gorce, 1986, pp. 56–57
Nationalmuseum, Stockholm, THC 924

This drawing is a presentation piece worked up from Berain's sketches by his workshop. It was sent to Stockholm on August 14, 1696. The upper part shows a baldachin, from which is suspended a cloth, raised on each side by a winged satyr. On the center of the cloth is a crowned shield bearing the monogram of Charles XI in red chalk; below, in the middle of the drawing, is the figure of Victory with flags. In the center of the lower part (on a gold background with stars), Hercules supports a globe decorated with three crowns, the arms of the Swedish kingdom. He is flanked by Justice and Prudence; lions lie by each of these female allegories. This sheet gives some idea of the symbolic program devised by Berain for the coach.
A.T.-J. and G.W.

69.

70.

70.
Unknown Draftsman
France, 1696
Carriage of the Duchesse d'Orléans for the Marriage of the Duc de Chartres
Black chalk, yellow and red wash; 92.2 × 58.4 cm.
Bibliography: For early references see Paris, 1985, no. R10; Tydén-
    Jordan, 1985; Stockholm, 1986, no. 80
Nationalmuseum, Stockholm, THC 947

When Tessin began to investigate the matter of a new state
coach after the stable fire of 1696, a problem arose. No truly
modern state coaches had been made in France for some
time. The best Cronström could find was the one shown in
this drawing of five years earlier. Although the design was not
thought suitable for the Swedish court, Cronström remarked,
"Its ornament in yellow leather and embroidery is in extremely good taste and executed as beautifully as can be
imagined" (Weigert and Hernmarck, 1964, p. 130). This
drawing was commissioned by Cronström and sent to Stockholm in 1696.
G.W.

71.
Unknown Draftsman
France, 1696
Carriage of the Duchesse d'Orléans: Front and Back
Black chalk, yellow, red, brown, and gray wash; 91 × 60.5 cm.
Bibliography: For early references see Paris, 1985, no. R11; Tydén-
    Jordan, 1985; Stockholm, 1986, no. 80a
Nationalmuseum, Stockholm, THC 946

72–75.
Unknown Draftsman
France, 1699
Uniforms of the Household of Louis XIV
Pen and black ink, watercolor; 30.4 × 21.4; 30.2 × 21.2; 29.5 ×
    20.5; 30.5 × 21.6 cm.
Inscribed with titles below
Bibliography: Josephson, 1938, I, pl. 163; Paris, 1951, nos. 99–102;
    Paris, 1985, nos. S1–S4; Stockholm, 1986, nos. 68–71
Nationalmuseum, Stockholm, THC 1394–1397

In a letter of 1699, Tessin wrote: "His Majesty [Charles XII]
is very curious to be informed of everything about the French
court, and in response to what he has been asking me, I
believe it would give him great pleasure to have made for him
rather large colored drawings of the dress of the royal household, especially the Grand Musketeers and the King's
Bodyguards, they must be done with exactitude" (Weigert
and Hernmarck, 1964, p. 216). Cronström immediately ordered the four drawings shown here. Their subjects are:
Grand Musketeer, mounted, accompanying the king (72);
Grand Musketeer in a guard's dress (73); the king's bodyguard, mounted, to follow the carriage of the king (74); the
king's bodyguard, unmounted (75).
G.W.

71.

Grand Mousquetaire à la Suitte du Roy.

72.

Grand Mousquetaire en Sentinelle.

73.

Garde du Corps suivant le Carosse du Roy

74.

Garde du Corps en faction.

75.

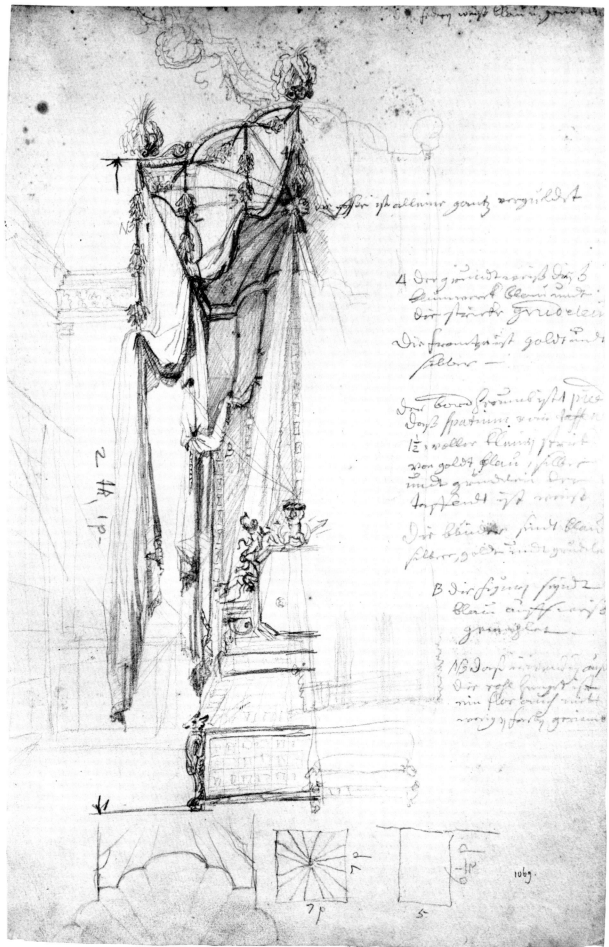

76.

1071.

76.
Nicodemus Tessin the Younger (1654–1728)
Sweden
Bed
Black chalk; 43 × 28.2 cm.
Inscribed throughout
Bibliography: Thornton, 1984, p. 57, fig. 62; Paris, 1985, no. K8
Nationalmuseum, Stockholm, THC 1069

This is one in an important series of studies of French beds
made by Tessin from notes taken during his second trip to
France in 1687. Many notes in German on color and materials
are found on the sheet. For the most part, beds were of little
interest to Tessin, although he did collect drawings of embroidery patterns for bed hangings. The bed in this drawing,
however, differed from the standard type of the time. The
novelty was the ornamental canopy top, which did not close
around the bed. The sketches across the lower portion of the
sheet include canopy studies. Later, in Sweden, Tessin designed a number of similar beds, such as one for Steninge
Castle now in the Nordiska Museet, Stockholm.

In all probability, Tessin found this bed at the Trianon de
Porcelaine at Versailles. That context would explain the
unusual shape of the piece, since the Trianon beds were *lits de
repos*—beds for naps, not for the night. The bed measured
6½ by 5 feet.

Though limited, the indication of the room's architectural
detail in this drawing is important, since no other view of the
interior of the building exists. Thornton believes that the
bed was Mme de Montespan's and was located in the Chambre de Diane.
G.W.

78.

77.
Nicodemus Tessin the Younger (1654–1728)
Sweden
Versailles: Bed from the Chambre des Amours at the Trianon de Porcelaine
Black chalk; 41.5 × 28.2 cm.
Inscribed throughout
Bibliography: A. and J. Marie, 1976, p. 555, fig. 210; Thornton, 1978,
    pp. 18, 402; Thornton, 1984, p. 57, fig. 61; Paris, 1985, no. K9
Nationalmuseum, Stockholm, THC 1071

Inventory descriptions identify this bed as one installed at
the Trianon de Porcelaine in 1672. It measured 6 by 5 French
feet. The inventory also mentions that a large mirror was set
at the head of the bed. Gray and silver ribbons were held by
papier-mâché putti, and the curtains were in white taffeta
embroidered with blue-gray linen, gold, and silver. The
furnishings of the bedchamber included four *carreaux*, four
large armchairs, four *portières*, and a table with flanking
candlestands.

Tessin drew the bed a few weeks before the destruction of
this garden palace to make way for the Grand Trianon in 1687.
G.W.

79.

80.

78.
Nicodemus Tessin the Younger (1654–1728)
Sweden
Bed
Black chalk; 40.9 × 27.3 cm.
Bibliography: Thornton, 1978, p. 18, fig. 15; Paris, 1985, no. K10
Nationalmuseum, THC 1070

Peter Thornton suggests that this bed, too, may have been at the Trianon de Porcelaine. In that case it would have been a third one, unmentioned in the inventories.
G.W.

79.
Nicodemus Tessin the Younger (1654–1728)
Sweden
Corner Ornament for the Foot of a Bed
Graphite; 27.5 × 20.2 cm.
Bibliography: Paris, 1985, no. K11
Nationalmuseum, Stockholm, THC 1072

This drawing is a study in detail of a corner of the bed in the previous drawing. The highly finished character of this and the previous sheet indicates that they were presentation drawings rather than notes from Tessin's visit. One cannot completely exclude the possibility that this is Tessin's own design, but it is more likely to be a polished reworking of a drawing he made in France.
G.W.

80.
Carl Hårleman ? (1700–1753)
Sweden
Candlestand
Pen and black ink, gray wash; 46.5 × 28 cm.
Bibliography: Paris, 1951, no. 118; Thornton, 1984, p.53, fig. 57; Paris, 1985, no. M8
Nationalmuseum, Stockholm, THC 8540

Carl Hårleman, later the royal architect of Sweden, spent the years from 1721 to 1725 in Paris working at the Académie Royale d'Architecture under Claude Desgots and Jacques Cazés and collecting and copying drawings. This drawing appears to be a rendering of a candlestand in a royal residence, perhaps Versailles. The intertwined *L*s and fleurs-de-lis are clearly distinguishable.

The motif of the globe showing the three fleurs-de-lis is of special interest. A royal order of December 22, 1688, states: "No. 460—8 large candlestands five feet three inches high made of sculpted wood and gilded, the arms of France repeated three times [on different sides of] a crowned globe, also made for the Great Gallery [Hall of Mirrors]" (J. Guiffrey, *Inventaire . . .*, Paris, 1885–86, II, p. 170). Although the globe in this drawing is not crowned, a circlet of ostrich feathers suggests that this is a work for the Dauphin. The design, nonetheless, may relate to the 1688 commission, which Pierre Verlet has recently described (in "Les gueridons de la Galerie des Glaces," *B.S.H.A.F.*, 1985–87, p. 130) as possibly the king's secret preparation for the melting of Versailles' silver furniture. According to Verlet, however, this design was abandoned in favor of another. The piece is later in style than those by Ballin and relates more closely to

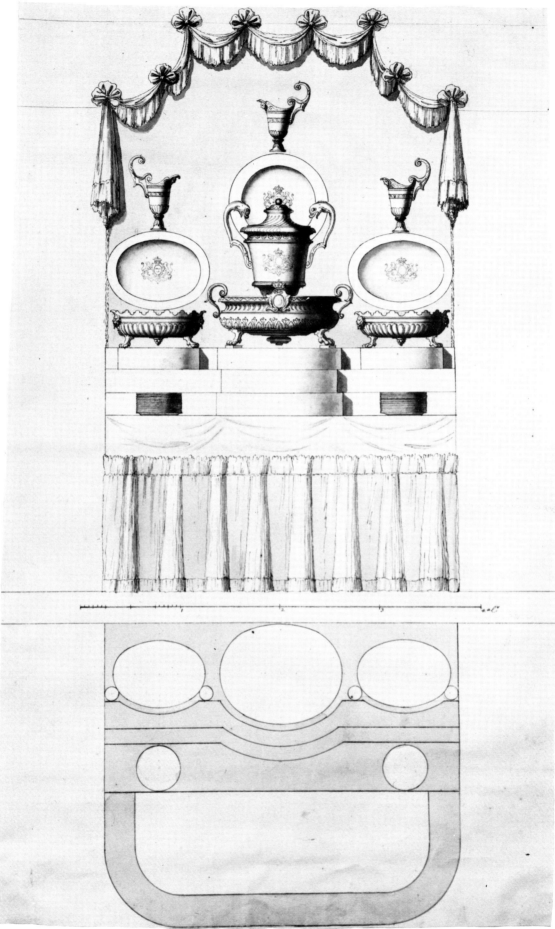

81.

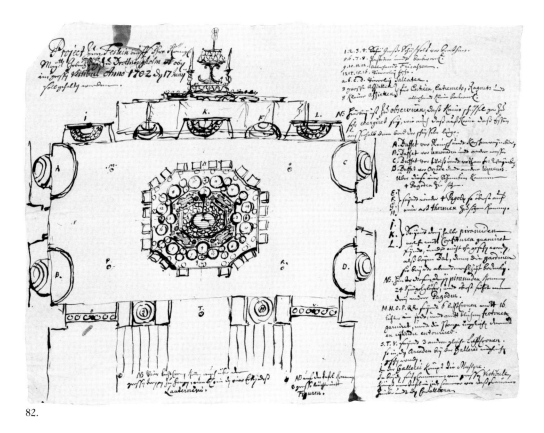

82.

designs by Jean Berain, suggesting a date of about 1690. Peter Thornton believes the drawing was done by Jean Berain for a suite of engravings recording the furniture in the State Apartment at Versailles.

This would have been a sheet Hårleman made for his notes—a work similar in function to the many drawings by Le Nôtre that he carefully copied while he worked in Desgots's workshop.

G.W.

81.
Workshop of Nicodemus Tessin the Younger (1654–1728)
Sweden
Arrangement of Silver Service for the Royal Household
Pen and black ink, gray wash; 44 × 26.2 cm
Bibliography: Josephson, 1938, II, pl. 179
Nationalmuseum, Stockholm, 54/1903

Descriptions in the correspondence between Cronström and Tessin and many drawings sent to Stockholm kept the Swedish royal family up to date concerning the French royal silver service. Tessin made use of all of this information. The pieces shown in the drawing relate closely to French examples (for instance, the pitcher can be compared to the Jean Berain design, No. 44).

The king himself (Charles XI), as Tessin wrote in 1694, found the French examples very beautiful. Tessin noted that the king was always particularly concerned about everything that pertained "to his own glory" (Weigert and Hernmarck, 1964, p.59).

E.E.D.

82.
Nicodemus Tessin the Younger (1654–1728)
Sweden
Table Setting at Drottningholm for Charles XII's Birthday
Pen and brown ink; 31 × 42 cm.
Inscribed: *Project für Festein . . . Konigs / Majsty Geburtz Tag in Drott-ningholm oby / im Grossy Vestibul Anno 1702 ad 17 Junÿ*; at right, key and identification
Bibliography: Josephson, 1938, II, pl. 171
Nationalmuseum, Stockholm, 49/1903

Tessin was concerned that every facet of the Swedish court's activities be conducted in a manner appropriate to the king's stature as monarch. No detail was too insignificant for the royal architect's attention, including exactly how the table should be set for the king's meal. As early as 1694, Cronström wrote from France that Jean Berain had promised to send the new style of festive table settings, service, and buffets. Tessin was still pursuing specific information in this connection several years later, as the drawing of the table setting at Marly dated 1700 verifies (see No. 37).

The inscription at the upper left of this drawing identifies the occasion for the diagram with its lengthy instructions as a birthday party in honor of Charles XII (who had succeeded his father in 1697) on June 17, 1702. It took place at the royal palace of Drottningholm, outside Stockholm.

E.E.D.

83.
Workshop of Nicodemus Tessin the Younger (1654–1728)
Sweden
Tessin Palace: Elevation, Garden Façade
Pen and black ink, gray wash, graphite; 42.3 × 61.5 cm.
Bibliography: Josephson, 1938, I, pl. 127
Nationalmuseum, Stockholm, THC 1263

Tessin wrote to Cronström in January 1697 that he intended
to work on his own palace that year and hoped, "God willing," that he would be able to move in by Saint John's Day,
which is in June (Weigert and Hernmarck, 1964, p. 160).
Appropriately, the structure was located just opposite the
Royal Palace's south façade, where Tessin could gaze upon
his greatest architectural achievement with pride. From this
vantage point, he could conveniently supervise the many
phases of the palace's construction. The design of his own
residence, though on a smaller scale, is typical of Tessin's
approach to palace architecture. The exterior of the building
reflects Tessin's study of baroque palaces in Florence and
Rome, while the interior decoration, the arrangement of
rooms, and the layout of the flower beds in the garden are
based on French prototypes.

It was Tessin's idea that upon entering the palace from the
street, the visitor would be able to look straight through to
the garden court. The color scheme of the hall was a re-
strained gray and white, in imitation of stone and marble,
contrasting with the greenery and colorful flowers outside
and with the brilliant hues of the State Apartment upstairs.

An appropriate iconographic program for the interior decoration was devised by the architect, and in the letter cited
above, Tessin asked Cronström to find French painters who
could carry out the work over a period of two or three years.
The agent was successful as Jacques Fouquet, Jacques de
Meaux, and René Chauveau all participated in the interior
work at Tessin's residence as well as in that at the Royal
Palace. Tessin stipulated precisely that drawings, no doubt
his own, would be provided for the decorations.
E.E.D.

84.
Workshop of Nicodemus Tessin the Younger (1654–1728)
Sweden
Tessin Palace: Elevation, Garden Façade
Pen and black ink, gray wash; 43.6 × 57 cm.
Bibliography: Josephson, 1938, I, pl. 126; Stockholm, 1978, no. 10
Nationalmuseum, Stockholm, THC 1264

The overall plan of the Tessin Palace was roughly triangular,
with the two story wings projecting at either side of the
garden from the main three-story, rectangular building. The
wings were connected at the end of the parterre by a narrow,
colonnaded passageway with a semicircular diversion at the
center. The shape of the plan was determined by the surrounding properties and Tessin tried not only to screen out
the neighboring buildings but, through exterior painting and
reliefs, to create the illusion of greater space. The most
remarkable of these devices, visible in the drawing, is on the
upper exterior wall of the connecting passageway: a relief in
perspective of a columned hall that, like a Bibiena stage
design, seems to retreat into a vast distance.

83.

84.

The ground floors of the wings were originally open arcades on the walls of which garden landscapes were painted. The enclosed garden was in the formal French manner, with plants and colored sands arranged in a pattern resembling embroidery. At the far end Tessin planned a grotto, similar to those he had seen in Italy, which could be used as a retreat for quiet meditation; significantly, its entrance was flanked by sculptures of philosophers. The grotto was provided with a murmuring fountain and a bed made of branches covered with a silk fabric painted to simulate straw. To further block out views of adjoining structures, Tessin planned to place cut-out sheet-iron trees on the roof of each wing.
E.E.D.

85.
René Chauveau (1663–1722)
France
Tessin Palace: Ceiling for the Salon
Pen and gray/black ink, watercolor, gold paint; 59.5 × 69.8 cm.
Bibliography: F. U. Wrangel, *Tessinska palatset*, Stockholm, 1912, pp. 11–12, pls. 17–20; Stockholm, 1978, no. 11; Stockholm, 1986, no. 137
Nationalmuseum, Stockholm, THC 5651

The running theme of the painted and sculpted decorations of the Tessin Palace was the personification of the arts and sciences. As at Versailles, Apollo, the sun god, figures prominently. In this drawing of the salon ceiling Apollo, splendidly illuminated and surrounded by nine muses, occupies the central medallion. Most revealing of Tessin's personality and philosophy is the iconographic program of the entire ceiling with allegorical figures and inscriptions around the Apollo group. Theory is contrasted with Action at opposite ends of the medallion. At the center of one of the long sides is Idea, which is carried out by Drawing on the opposite side. In the corners are Engineering, with a nearby pedestal naming Domenico Fontana as Tessin's choice for its supreme representative; Architecture, naming Bramante and Bernini; Sculpture, naming Michelangelo and Algardi; and Painting, naming Raphael and Annibale Carracci. The drawings for the ceiling were made by Chauveau, carrying out Tessin's program.

The remaining decoration of the room, as on the painted exterior of the palace, is a play between illusion and reality. The walls seem to disappear by means of two views of Italian landscapes showing Mount Vesuvius erupting and the cascades of Tivoli. Illusion is carried further by the real and the painted draperies in the same color of red.
E.E.D.

86–87.
Attributed to Jacques de Meaux
France, c. 1700
Two Vases, Each on a Console
Sanguine, yellow and red wash; each 34 × 20.5 cm.
Bibliography: Paris, 1985, nos. P4, P5
Nationalmuseum, Stockholm, THC 823, 825

These two drawings are from a group executed in sanguine and yellow wash. Two of the compositions from the group appear in an ornamental painting on the wall of the state bedroom of Tessin's palace. Since Jacques de Meaux is

86.

87.

85.

known to have worked there, it is possible that he did the decorations and these drawings.

Both of the objects shown here are clearly in the style of Berain's consoles— which suggests the considerable degree of refinement of the French and Swedish decorators' work both at the Stockholm Royal Palace and at Tessin's home.

The room also included a ceiling painting with a composition centered on Day and Night adapted from a ceiling painting at the Villa Caprarola near Rome, and a large illusionistic wall painting simulating a theater stage. The head of Diana, the moon goddess appears on No. 86.
G.W.

88.

88.
Attributed to Jacques de Meaux
France, c. 1700
Gilt Pitcher on a Console
Sanguine, yellow and red wash; 47 × 25.6 cm.
Bibliography: Paris, 1985, no. P6
Nationalmuseum, Stockholm, THC 824

Agneta Börtz-Laine has recognized that the object depicted here appears in the wall decoration of the state bedroom of Tessin's palace. The manner in which it was incorporated into that design explains the curious flaired bottom of the console, which fits within a frame of grotesque ornament. This object appears twice in the painting, with one image in reverse of the other.
G.W.

89.
Attributed to Jacques de Meaux
France, c. 1700
Gilt Perfume Burner or Brazier
Sanguine, yellow and red wash; 47 × 34.5 cm.
Bibliography: Thornton, 1978, p. 326, fig. 318; Paris, 1985, no. P7
Nationalmuseum, Stockholm, THC 826

This extraordinary object was once thought by Peter Thornton to be an important piece of French silver furniture. Agneta Börtz-Laine pointed out that it is, rather, the object in the center of the decorative wall panel in the state bedroom of Tessin's palace. The painting is a mixture of Berainesque grotesques and antique ornament, but this particular object is very much of its time, about 1700. Attractive as it is, it cannot claim to meet the best standard of French silver design. Actual objects such as that depicted here were part of the decoration of sumptuous seventeenth-century palaces like Versailles. A clock design with the arms of the Swedish king by the same hand is also in the Nationalmuseum collection.
G.W.

89.

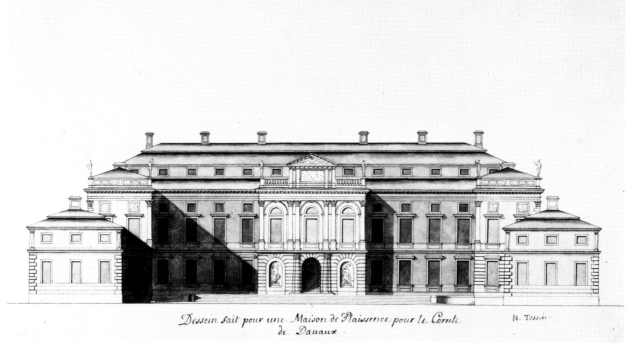

Dessein fait pour une Maison de Plaissence pour le Comte de Dauaux.

N. Tessin.

90.

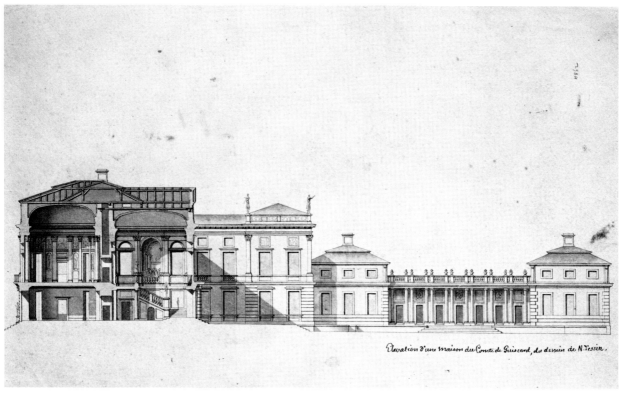

Elevation d'une maison du Comte de Guiscard, du dessein de N. Tessin.

91.

90.
Workshop of Nicodemus Tessin the Younger (1654–1728)
Sweden
Château de Roissy-en-France: Elevation, Main Façade
Pen and black ink, watercolor; 26.5 × 41.3 cm.
Inscribed: *Dessein fait pour une Maison de Plaissence pour le Comte / de Danaux / N. Tessin*
Bibliography: Josephson, 1930, pp. 35–46, pl. vi; Josephson, 1938, pl. 133
Nationalmuseum, Stockholm, THC 2401

Count d'Avaux, the French envoy in Sweden, engaged Tessin late in 1697 for the construction of a new château on some family property in Ile-de-France, originally the seat of the monarchy. The chief proprietor of the estate was Jean-Jacques de Mesmes, president of the parliament in Paris. Tessin, who had been eager to have his name and work known in France, was overjoyed to accept the commission. In his usual efficient method of operation, he had the preliminary designs ready in the spring of 1698 and the presentation drawings in June. Construction was underway in 1700, and the building was almost finished by 1704. By 1796, however, it is recorded that the château had fallen into ruin, and no trace of it has remained. It is one of the most well documented of Tessin's projects. Since he was in Sweden, discussions and changes to the plans were carried out through correspondence between the architect and the client, and these letters have been preserved along with the drawings. The château consisted of a central building flanked by two wings, which in turn were connected with two lower structures. These enclosed a courtyard with an iron grill across one end. The style of the façades, with rusticated stone pilasters with Corinthian capitals in the corners, and rich ornamentation of the central entrance section—relates to Italian palaces Tessin had studied. The most original element of the design was the double pitch of the roof, which was based on Swedish architectural traditions. This roof type was unknown in France and prompted Hardouin-Mansart, the French royal architect, who approved of the design otherwise, to say, "The roof seems bizarre . . . but I am sure there is a reason to make it this way."
E.E.D.

91.
Workshop of Nicodemus Tessin the Younger (1654–1728)
Sweden
Château de Roissy-en-France: Elevation and Section
Pen and black ink, gray, blue, and rose wash; 25.3 × 41.7 cm.
Inscribed: *Elevation d'une Maison du Comte de Guiscard, du dessein de N. Tessin*
Bibliography: Josephson, 1930, pl. vii; Josephson, 1938, II, pl. 134
Nationalmuseum, Stockholm, THC 4862

Tessin originally planned an immense double stairway for the main entrance at Roissy, probably influenced by the Stairway of the Ambassadors at Versailles, that was to lead to an oval salon. In the final version, however, the stairway, still imposing in size, was placed to the right.
E.E.D.

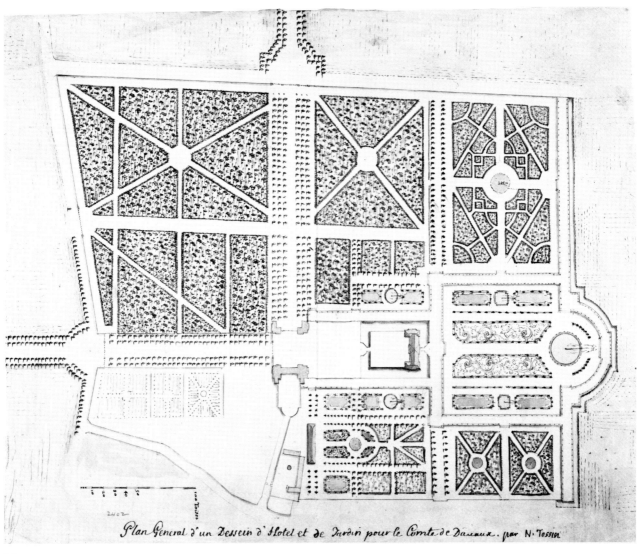

Plan Général d'un Dessein d'Hôtel et de Jardin pour le Comte de Daueaux. par N. Tessin

92.

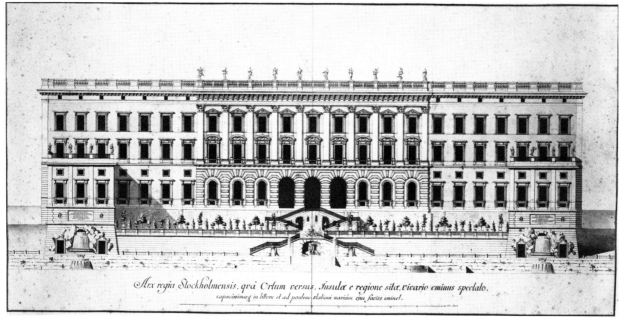

Arx regia Stockholmensis, qva Ortum versus, Insulæ e regione sitæ, vivario eminus spectato, capacissimæq in littore et ad pontem stationi navium ejus facies eminet.

93.

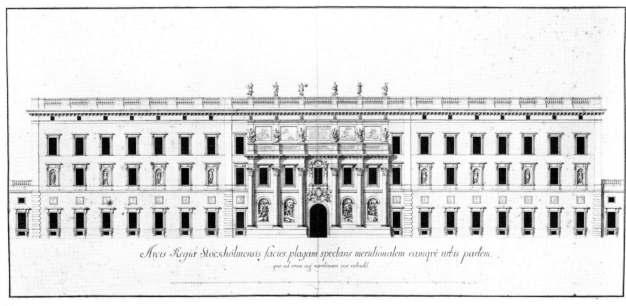

Arcis Regiæ Stockholmensis facies, plagam spectans meridionalem eamqvè urbis partem, qvæ ad oram usq maritimam sese extendit.

94.

92.
Workshop of Nicodemus Tessin the Younger (1654–1728)
Sweden
Château de Roissy-en-France: Plan of the Gardens
Pen and red and black ink, watercolor; 32 × 41 cm.
Inscribed: *Plan General d'un Dessein d'Hotel et de Jardin pour le Comte de
    Danaux par N. Tessin*
Bibliography: Josephson, 1930, pl. vii
Nationalmuseum, Stockholm, THC 2402

As is evident on the plan, the gardens surrounding the
château were extensive, with parterres, fountains, pools,
and wooded areas. The approach to the château from the
north—down a long allée with a triple row of trees at either
side—must have been impressive.
E.E.D.

93.
Workshop of Nicodemus Tessin the Younger (1654–1728)
Sweden
Royal Palace, Stockholm: Elevation of the East Façade
Pen and black ink; 44.2 × 88.2 cm.
Inscribed: *Arx regia Stockholmensis quà Ortum versus Insulae regione
    sitae, vivario eminus spectato . . .*
Bibliography: *S.S.H.*, II, pl. 30; Kommer, 1974, no. 35
Royal Palace, Stockholm, SAK 3, p.333

According to his memoirs, Tessin began to work on designs
for the expansion of the Royal Palace in Stockholm soon after
his return to Sweden from Europe in 1688. In 1681, following
his father's death, he had become the architect for the palace.

Although Tessin the Younger's vision was always for a
palace that would express the glory and majesty of the royal
family, his plans for the building evolved over a series of
years. At first, parts of the medieval palace were to be retained and refaced with a classical façade, but by 1692 Tessin
had abandoned that idea and presented plans for a completely new north wing. Meanwhile, in highly organized
fashion, he had ordered the gathering of the construction
materials and had the window frames and ornaments hewn so
that the wing was finished in 1694. On May 7, 1697, a disas-
trous fire demolished the entire palace except for the new
north wing. Tessin, however, was ready with new plans,
which were accepted within weeks. These, of course, were
revised many times over the next several years.

The site—on a hill, irregular, surrounded by the city, and
facing a large body of water—was a challenge to the architect. Tessin once again called upon his memories of Italian
villas situated on high land. The general appearance of the
Royal Palace exterior was based on Italian models, particularly Bernini's designs for the Louvre. Each façade has a
distinct character. At the north, the window placements
create a rhythmic pattern, and the ramps, like those at the
Villa Caprarola, are Tessin's solution to the problem of
providing an easy entrance on the sharp incline. The east
wing, on the water, is ornamented by make-believe grottoes
with artificial waterfalls, double stairs, and sculpture on the
theme of Ovid's *Metamorphoses*. The south wing, leading into
the ceremonial rooms, is richly ornamented with heroic
sculpture and bas-reliefs—the Labors of Hercules at the
lower level, trophies and allegorical reliefs above. The west
wing is more classical and refined with herms and Corinthian
capitals.
E.E.D.

95.

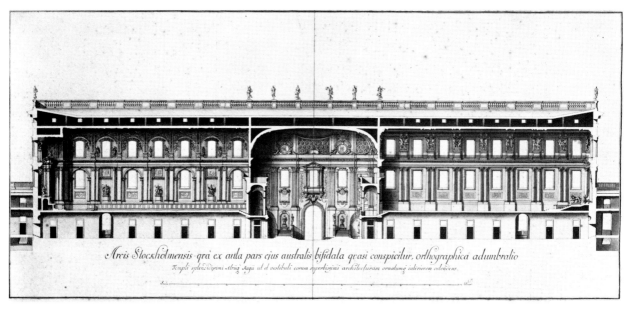

Arcis Stockholmensis quà ex aula pars ejus australis bifidala quasi conspicitur, orthographica adumbratio

Templi splendidissimi Atrÿ Regÿ ut et vestibuli eorum superbÿssimi architecturam ornatumÿ interiorem ostendens.

96.

94.
Workshop of Nicodemus Tessin the Younger (1654–1728)
Sweden
Royal Palace, Stockholm: Elevation of the South Façade
Pen and black ink, gray wash; 37.4 × 80 cm.
Inscribed: _Arcis Regiae Stockholmensis facies, plagam spectans merid-
ionalem eamquè urbis partem . . ._
Bibliography: _S.S.H._, II, pl. 28; Kommer, 1974, no. 31
Royal Palace, Stockholm, SAK 3, p.328

95.
Workshop of Nicodemus Tessin the Younger (1654–1728)
Sweden
Royal Palace, Stockholm: Detail of the South Façade
Pen and black ink, gray wash; 132 × 65.5 cm.
Bibliography: _S.S.H._, II, pp. 69–170, pl. 32; Kommer, 1974, no. 22
Royal Palace, Stockholm, SAK 4, p.338

96.
Workshop of Nicodemus Tessin the Younger (1654–1728)
Sweden
Royal Palace, Stockholm: Section of the South Wing
Pen and black ink, gray wash; 37.7 × 80.2 cm.
Inscribed: _Arcis Stockholmensis quà ex aula pars eius australis bifidata
quasi conspicitur, orthographica adumbratio . . ._
Bibliography: _S.S.H._, II, pl. 23b,; Kommer, 1974, no. 32
Royal Palace, Stockholm, SAK 3, p.330

The interiors of the royal Swedish residence followed the
pattern of Versailles—guard room, reception room, audience
room with tribune, bedroom with bed of state, and a small
private parlor. The ceremonial rooms on the upper story were
more brilliantly and richly ornamented with sculpted and

painted ornament describing the virtues and triumphs of the
royal family. Tessin's genius is revealed in the graceful, rhythmic way the enormous interior spaces are interrelated.
E.E.D.

97.
Nicodemus Tessin the Younger (1654–1728)
Sweden
_Royal Palace, Stockholm: Section Showing Details of the Hall of State and
the Chapel_
Graphite; 20.3 × 31.3 cm.
Inscribed throughout
Bibliography: _S.S.H._, II, p. 86, pl. 25a; Kommer, 1974, no. 23
Nationalmuseum, Stockholm, CC 757

98.
Workshop of Nicodemus Tessin the Younger (1654–1728)
Sweden
The Louvre, Paris: First Project, Circular Court Arcade
Pen and black ink, gray and black wash; 90 × 33.9 cm.
Bibliography: Josephson, 1930, pl. XV
Nationalmuseum, Stockholm, THC 1247

As early as 1660, Louis XIV's able finance minister, Jean-
Baptiste Colbert, had urged the king to make a monumental
complex uniting the Louvre and the Tuileries palaces. At the
king's request, a number of architects had contributed designs, including such notables as Louis Le Vau, Gianlorenzo
Bernini, and Claude Perrault, but their plans were either
rejected or only partially carried out.

In the beginning of 1703, rumors began to circulate that
Louis XIV intended to move the court from Versailles to Paris

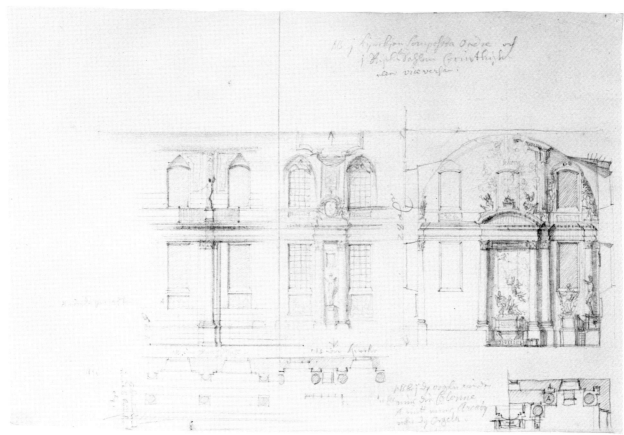

97.

and would therefore be more interested in continuing the construction of the Louvre. A year later, Tessin wrote to Cronström that he had been formulating ideas for the expansion of the Louvre and had begun to translate them to drawings. Determined to make his presentation by means of a model as well as drawings, Tessin sent a former student, Göran Josua Törnqvist Adelcrantz, to undertake the project of fabricating the model in France. When a formal viewing of the drawings and model finally took place, the king pronounced it in "great taste, very regular, very correct." The project, however, then had to run the gauntlet of French architects and the Académie Royale d'Architecture. It was roundly criticized, perhaps partly in jealousy.

Tessin's plans did not radically revise the north, south, and east façades; his innovations were concerned with the courtyard and the west wing. He proposed a huge forecourt in front of the east façade and a circular rather than square courtyard (the *cour carré*), an audacious suggestion that would have done away with an already existing building. The circular court was conceived as an amphitheater, open to the sky, with balconies where spectators could attend carrousels and fêtes of all sorts.

The grandiose character of Tessin's plan becomes apparent through his own detailed description of the project in which he estimates that between twenty and twenty-five thousand spectators could be accommodated. The façades surrounding the courtyard were ornamented with sculptures, similar in concept to those Tessin commissioned for the Royal Palace in Stockholm. He himself made drawings for the sixty-four medallions representing the kings of France that were to be placed in the frieze of the ground floor.
E.E.D.

99.
Nicodemus Tessin the Younger (1654–1728)
Sweden
The Louvre, Paris: Second Project, Plan and Section of the West Wing
Pen and brown ink; 32 × 21 cm.
Inscribed throughout
Nationalmuseum, Stockholm, THC 1258:120

Regrettably for Tessin, Louis XIV did not appear to be in haste to expand the Louvre. The lack of momentum and the rather harsh judgments on his design might have deterred a less ambitious and imaginative architect, but in 1706 Tessin was enthusiastically creating new designs that responded to the criticisms of the first. He abandoned the circular courtyard, but retained the idea of surrounding the square courtyard with galleries. Many other changes were made as well, and the garden terraces and flights of stairs connecting the two palaces—considered the most successful element of his designs—received still more attention.
E.E.D.

98.

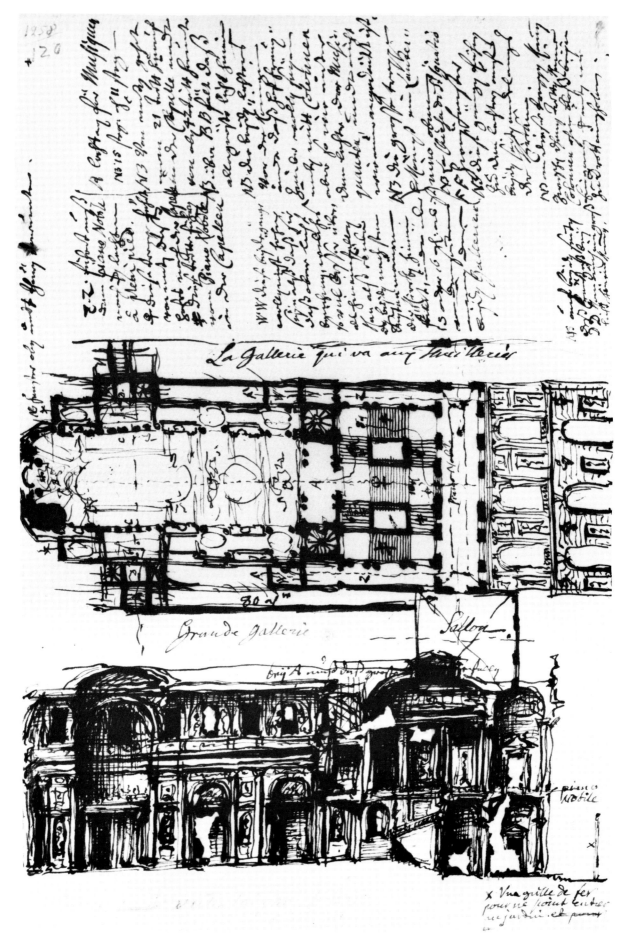

La Gallerie qui va aux Thuilleries

Grande gallerie

Sallon

99.

100.

100.
Workshop of Nicodemus Tessin the Younger (1654–1728)
Sweden
The Louvre, Paris: Second Project, Elevation and Section of the West Wing
Pen and black ink, gray and black wash, 25.7 × 46 cm.
Bibliography: Josephson, 1930, pl. XVIII
Nationalmuseum, Stockholm, THC 1246

The presentation of Tessin's second project for the Louvre took place in Paris in 1714, and was made by the architect's son Carl Gustaf. No attempt was made to have a second model created; for the presentation to the king and others, there were just the magnificent drawings by Tessin and presentation drawings after them, probably by his draftsman, Carl Palmcrantz (1694–1715).

The time was not propitious for such a vast building program. France had been at war until 1713, and by 1714, even the most optimistic architect would regard his proposal as mainly a paper exercise in the glorification of the king. Louis, an aging monarch whose reign was nearly over, showed Tessin's designs to his great-grandson (who was to succeed him as Louis XV), but to no avail.
E.E.D.

101.
Nicodemus Tessin the Younger (1654–1728)
Sweden
Palace in the Country (Lustslott) for Charles XII: Plan, Façade, and Section
Pen and brown ink, gray wash; 33.4 × 40 cm.
Bibliography: Josephson, 1938, II, pp. 106–9, pl. 67; Stockholm, 1978, no. 25; Margareta Reuterskiöld, "Den sista stormaktsdrömmen," *Konsthistorisk tidskrift* 49: fig. 3
Nationalmuseum, Stockholm, THC 1550b:13

Although the circular court for the Louvre was rejected, Tessin found another outlet for the idea in his plans for a country palace for Charles XII. The drawings were sent in 1712 to the king in Bender, Turkey, where he was plotting his second—and as it turned out, unsuccessful—military campaign against Peter the Great of Russia.

Numerous drawings for the project in Tessin's lively pen work exist and provide insight into the fertility of his ideas and the progressive stages of his work. He tended to move from complex to more contained architectural plans—perhaps at the request of his clients.

Typically, the architect conceptualized on a grand scale when working for a royal patron. Thus, in what is apparently the first alternative for a country palace, Tessin includes a three-story oval structure in the center, with arcaded galleries around a court. The palace as a whole is divided into sections surrounding four rectangular open courts with pools and fountains. It was intended that there would be space in these sections for libraries, medal cabinets, painting galleries, and billiard rooms.

In a later alternative, the oval was sliced in half, with a double stairway forming a semicircle of the façade. It appears that the palace was to be approached by water. Although the projected site is not known, some coastal area north of Stockholm seems most likely.
E.E.D.

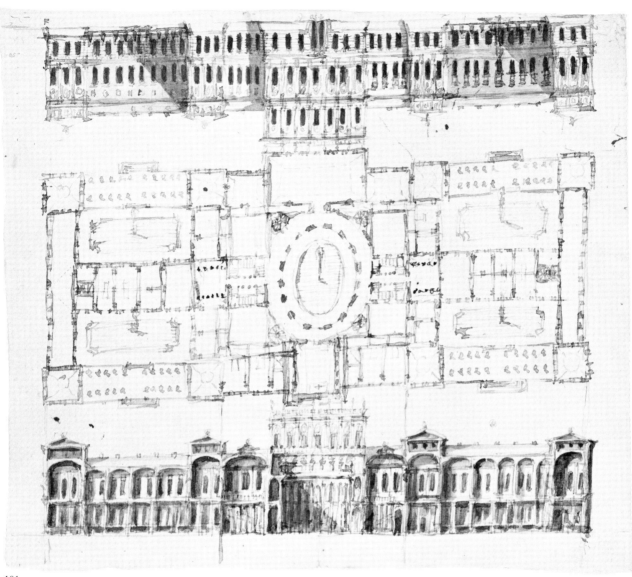

101.

103.

102.
Nicodemus Tessin the Younger (1654–1728)
Sweden
Palace in the Country for Charles XII: Detail of the Pavilion
Pen and brown ink, gray wash; 23 × 13.5 cm.
Inscribed: *L'Ornamento sera 2/9/A . . . Corniche vous . . . Ionique
    Order;* scale
Bibliography: Josephson, 1938, II, pl. 74
Nationalmuseum, Stockholm, THC 1550b:3

103.
Workshop of Nicodemus Tessin the Younger (1654–1728)
Sweden
Palace in the Country for Charles XII: Section Showing Stairwell
Pen and brown ink, brown and gray wash, black chalk; 22.8 × 26.7
    cm.
Inscribed: *. . . trappen fur den ovale / garten*
Bibliography: Josephson, 1938, II, pl. 68.; Stockholm, 1978, no. 27
Nationalmuseum, Stockholm, THC 1550b:9

104.
Nicodemus Tessin the Younger (1654–1728)
Sweden
Palace in the Country for Charles XII: Garden Plan
Pen and brown ink, watercolor; 281.5 × 56.5 cm.
Bibliography: Reuterskiöld, pp. 108–17, fig. 1
The Estate of Consul General Axel Ax:son Johnson, (W16)V22

The garden plan for Charles XII's country palace was nothing
short of fantastic, and the possibility that Tessin was aiming
for a Swedish Versailles is not beyond credibility.

   In this plan the pier in front of the palace is clearly visible.
The palace itself is roughly formed of a central square with
two wings that project from either side and enclose garden
courts. The gardens are varied, with every conceivable type
of planting and parterre. A cascade, fountains, and a large
amphitheater around a pool, as well as other pools, provided
the sound and sight of splashing water. Midway in the garden
was a rotunda for viewing or resting, and at the very end of
the expanse, adjacent to the amphitheater, was a small
theater.
E.E.D.

105.
Workshop of Nicodemus Tessin the Younger (1654–1728)
Sweden
Carrousel for Charles XII
Pen and black ink, gray wash; 36 × 51.5 cm.
Bibliography: Josephson, 1938, I, pl. 185
Nationalmuseum, Stockholm, THC 5320

Tessin sought out information from Europe concerning another form of royal entertainment enjoyed there, the carrousel. Through prints by Jacques Callot, Stefano della
Bella, and others, and the Berain drawings that Tessin ordered through Cronström, Swedish designers were aware of
how the carrousels were arranged and how they looked. A
carrousel consisted of chariots or floats, mechanically ani-
mated figures, a recitation on a chosen theme of some sort,
and always and most importantly, a horse ballet or quadrille.
The members of the court participated in these quadrilles
wearing specially created costumes (for a 1685 carrousel in

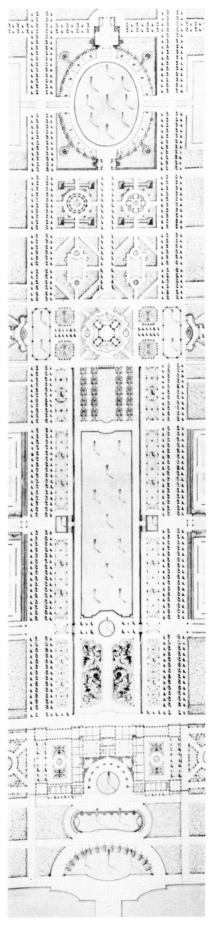

104.

105.

Project uf Ihb. Exm graf N. Tessin hee de Sallon D'appollons. — a Versailles

106.

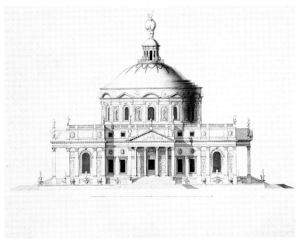

107.

France, eighty costumes were made). At Marly a theater was temporarily installed and dismantled for the carrousel there.

Because Charles XII stayed in Turkey for five years, it was necessary for Tessin to send drawings such as this to the king at regular intervals in order to keep the building programs in Stockholm flowing. Several plans for enlarging the royal stables were prepared and sent in 1712 to the king, who, commenting that the stable should be large enough to house a carrousel, suggested that the design be expanded.

The carrousel of 1713 in this drawing prepared by Tessin is documented through several drawings in the Nationalmuseum, and it included, along with the horse ballet, a dragon chariot that puffed smoke and another chariot, simulating a rocky crag, drawn by centaurs. A warrior hero, triumphant over captives strewn below him, stood on the rocks—very likely an allusion to the hoped-for triumphs of the Swedish king.

E.E.D.

106.
Nicodemus Tessin the Younger (1654–1728)
Sweden, 1654–1728
Versailles: Apollo Pavilion, Project for the Façade
Pen and brown ink; 21.5 × 20.5 cm.
Inscribed: *Project af Hs Exce Graf N. Tessin till Le Sallon / D'apollon Versailles*
Bibliography: For early references see Paris, 1985, no. L1
Nationalmuseum, Stockholm, Celsing 122

On April 9, 1712, Tessin wrote, "Three months ago I conceived a grand project for a salon of mirrors in the middle of a pavilion dedicated to Apollo." During the summer of 1714 Tessin wrote to Cronström in France that his son would bring the project with him to Paris. This structure—a garden pavilion combined with a museum—was to be a kind of homage to the accomplishments in the arts of the Sun King. Tessin realized that the time was not right, given Louis's age and the state of France, for the realization of the project, but he hoped that his son, by presenting it to the king, would meet with a cordial reception in France. Louis XIV died before the presentation could be accomplished.

Most of the surviving drawings for this project in Stockholm are by Carl Palmcrantz (1694–1715). This grand exterior elevation is the only major drawing for the exterior from the architect's own hand that has survived. The vigorous pen work gives some sense of the liveliness of Tessin's imagination and contrasts strongly with the handling in the drawings from his workshop.

A.B.-L. and G.W.

107.
Carl Palmcrantz (1694–1715) after Nicodemus Tessin the Younger (1654–1728)
Sweden
Versailles: Apollo Pavilion, Façade
Pen and black ink, gray wash; 35.5 × 51.3 cm.
Bibliography: For early references see Paris, 1985, L2; Walton, 1986, fig. 151
Nationalmuseum, Stockholm, THC 1199

Since Tessin considered it possible that the Apollo Pavilion would be located at the end of the canal of Versailles, about two kilometers from the château, the work was conceived as a very large building 90 meters wide and 53 meters high. It would have been built of white marble with reliefs in marble and in gilt bronze—the only materials, according to Tessin, that would do for such an important project. The tympanum was to show Minerva (goddess of wisdom) and the Muses. Reliefs above these would depict the Virtues and the symbols of the monarch who had been a great patron of the arts. On top of the dome was to be a figure of Apollo seated on the celestial globe, supported by Atlas.

In keeping with the idea that the pavilion temple was both a tribute to Apollo and to the art of architecture, its design recalls the Pantheon in Rome, Palladio's Villa Rotonda, and other architectural classics.
A. B.-L. and G.W.

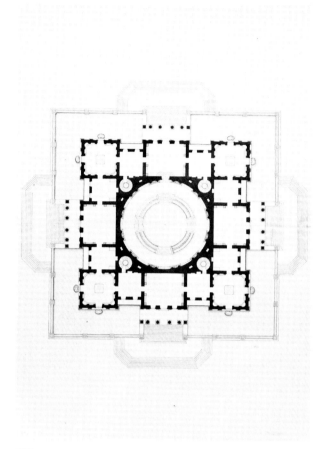

108.
Carl Palmcrantz (1694–1715) after Nicodemus Tessin the Younger
(1654–1728)
Sweden
Versailles: Apollo Pavilion, Plan
Pen and black ink, gray and blue wash; 68.6 × 46.7 cm.
Bibliography: For early references see Paris, 1985, L3
Nationalmuseum, Stockholm, THC 1201

The arrangement of the interior of Tessin's Apollo Pavilion is suggested by this plan. The four corner rooms would have been galleries or curiosity cabinets. Busts of principal figures in the sciences and the arts would have been placed in other outside rooms. Small rooms would serve as lounges. The resemblance to the plan of the Château de Marly (No. 23) is noteworthy.
A.B.-L. and G.W.

108.

109.
Carl Palmcrantz (1694–1715) after Nicodemus Tessin the Younger
(1654–1728)
Sweden
Versailles: Apollo Pavilion, Section
Pen and black ink, gray wash; 35.4 × 51.3 cm.
Bibliography: For early references see Paris, 1985, L4
Nationalmuseum, Stockholm, THC 1200

The decor of the pavilion's central Salon of Apollo shows a remarkable fusion of Italian and French ideas characteristic of Tessin, who admired aspects of each school. The coffering of the dome is a variant of that in Bernini's San Andrea al Quirinale, while the mirrored walls suggest various French interiors, particularly at Versailles. The architect was especially proud of the indirect lighting, which he thought would be novel and apropos for the Sun King. The use of a fountain, a highly original feature in the context of the mirrored walls, in the middle of the room recalls Louis XIV's bath (No. 7).

Tessin's description of the room gives some sense of its meaning to him: "Since the sun is at its greatest strength when it is highest in the sky it would seem that light from above is preferable to any other kind . . . . This light is that which is esteemed in Italy . . . . At the rotunda [the Pantheon] in Rome one notices that every detail is enhanced by

109.

110.

. . . the light . . . and since there is nowhere in the world where novelty is more appreciated than in Paris, I am sure that if a salon of this type could actually be constructed the effect of it would surpass what many could imagine."
G.W.

110.
Carl Palmcrantz (1694–1715) after Nicodemus Tessin the Younger (1654–1728)
Sweden
Versailles: Apollo Pavilion, Wall Decoration, Salon of Apollo
Pen and black ink, gray wash; 92.48 × 66 cm.
Bibliography: For early references see Paris, 1985, L5
Nationalmuseum, Stockholm, THC 1202

The decorative elements shown in this design, such as the statues and the ornament with imagery including lyres and sphinxes, underscore the Apollo theme of the room. The statues of the months and of the first four hours of the day recall the complex, all-encompassing iconographic programs of the rooms and gardens of Versailles from the 1670s. Tessin must have carefully read the guide by André Félibien (1610–1695) in 1687 and paid careful attention while Le Nôtre explained the Versailles program to him.

Tessin's room, with antecedents in the architecture of Bernini and in the statue of *Winter* by Girardon, fuses French and Italian stylistic elements to create an absolutist grandeur of subtle refinement that is not limited to any single national tradition. Like Tessin's designs for the Louvre or his treatise on interior decoration, *Traité de la décoration interieur*, it is the product of a fine sensibility and employs a vocabulary of good design that could be understood by any talented European designer. Sweden's court architect felt that he was worthy to compete with any national tradition, even those of the great capitals of art, Rome and Paris.
A.B.-L. and G.W.